$10.95

Northwest Trees

British Columbia

WHITEBARK PINE

ALPINE LARCH

MOUNTAIN HEMLOCK

PACIFIC SILVER FIR

SUBALPINE FIR

WESTERN LARCH with LODGEPOLE PINE (medium elevations)

WESTERN HEMLOCK—DOUGLAS-FIR FOREST

ALASKA-CEDAR

PONDEROSA PINE (lower elevations)

ENGELMANN SPRUCE (near streams)

SITKA ALDER (snow slides)

Columbia Basin

GRAND FIR

DOUGLAS-FIR

WESTERN JUNIPER scattered among SAGEBRUSH

RED ALDER GROVES

ASPEN GROVES

WATER BIRCH

BLACK COTTON-WOOD

NOBLE FIR

WILLOWS

SUGAR PINE

GOLDEN CHINKAPIN

INCENSE-CEDAR

WESTERN JUNIPER

Oregon

NETLEAF HACKBERRY

Northwest

Trees

TEXT BY Stephen F. Arno

ART BY Ramona P. Hammerly

The Mountaineers

SEATTLE, WASHINGTON

THE MOUNTAINEERS: Organized 1906
". . . to explore, study, preserve and enjoy
the natural beauty of Northwest America . . ."

Copyright © 1977 by The Mountaineers. All rights reserved.

Published by The Mountaineers
719 Pike Street, Seattle, Washington 98101

Published simultaneously in Canada by
Douglas & McIntyre Ltd., 1875 Welch Street
North Vancouver, British Columbia V7P 1B7

Manufactured in the United States of America

Library of Congress Catalog Card No. 77-82369
ISBN 0-916890-50-3

First printing, October 1977
Second printing, September 1979

Acknowledgments

I would like to thank several people who reviewed this manu-
script and provided helpful comments: my first forestry profes-
sor, the late Dr. Roland Rethke; my parents, Mr. and Mrs. Sieg-
fried Arno; my wife Bonnie; Drs. R. F. Stettler and James N.
Long of the University of Washington, and T. C. Brayshaw of
the British Columbia Provincial Museum. Both Ramona Hammerly and I would like to thank John Pollock, Peggy Ferber,
Donna DeShazo, and Joan Firey, members of the Literary Fund
Committee of The Mountaineers, who provided encouragement
and managed most phases of this book's production.

STEPHEN F. ARNO

Introduction

This guidebook for discovering and understanding the re-markable trees and rich forests of the Northwest covers the area of southern British Columbia, Washington, the northern half of Oregon, northern Idaho, and northwestern Montana. The drawing on pages ii and iii depicts the composition of our forests and is suggested as a starting point.

Although the Pacific Maritime Forest extends 2500 miles from south-central Alaska to San Francisco, California, it reaches its optimum development in the Northwest area. This maritime forest zone, probably unequalled in volume of wood by any other forest of comparable area in the world, is made up of several outstanding species — including Sitka spruce, western hemlock, western redcedar, coastal Douglas-fir, and mountain hemlock — which thrive here but grow essentially nowhere else.

At its northern and southern extremities (in Alaska and California, respectively) this forest zone becomes narrow and is confined to the immediate coast. However, from southern British Columbia to northern Oregon, it is especially luxuriant and expands to cover most of the terrain between the ocean and the summit of the Cascades. Only in these latitudes does an arm of the maritime forest spill over the high mountains to occupy part of the interior — southeastern British Columbia, northeastern Washington, northern Idaho, and northwestern Montana.

Farther south, in southwestern Oregon and northern California, this forest merges with and gradually gives way to many new species of trees and shrubs whose major distributions lie in the warmer and drier climates of California. (At its southern end, it becomes the unique "redwood forest," occupying a narrow band in the coastal fog belt of northern California.) However, only three of the California species — sugar pine, incense-cedar, and golden chinkapin — extend north into the area covered by this book.

The Pacific Northwest is an area notable for tremendous climatic diversity: annual precipitation at low elevations ranges from about 150 inches in some of the coastal "rain forests" down to as little as 15 inches in parts of northern Puget Sound which lie in the rain-shadow of the Olympic Mountains. The wetter forests are dominated by Sitka spruce, western hemlock, and western redcedar, while the drier ones tend to be composed mostly of Douglas-fir, Pacific madrone, and even Oregon white oak. The high, snowy mountains are "another world" as far as trees are concerned, with a completely different assortment of interesting species.

Lower elevations east of the lofty Cascades are quite dry, with annual precipitation ranging down to a meager 6 inches (coupled with summer temperatures that reach 110 degrees F. or higher) in the Columbia Basin "desert." These harsh conditions cannot be tolerated by the coastal trees, but several inland and desert-dwelling species grow here along stream-courses and rocky canyon walls (examples include the junipers, peachleaf willow, and netleaf hackberry).

Still farther east in the Northwest lies a portion of the Rocky Mountains; these and other mountains east of the Cascade Crest harbor forest species (such as western larch, alpine larch; ponderosa, lodgepole, and whitebark pines; Engelmann spruce; and quaking aspen) that mix with Pacific conifers and add to the diversity of the forests.

The author, artist, and publisher hope this book will stimulate readers to investigate the broader subject of forest ecology. Many fine publications provide additional information; the following list makes a good starting point:

Hitchcock, C. L., A. Cronquist, M. Ownbey, and J. W. Thompson. 1955-69. Vascular plants of the Pacific Northwest. (5 vols.) Univ. Wash. Press, Seattle.

Hitchcock, C. L. and A. Cronquist. 1973. Flora of the Pacific Northwest. Univ. Wash. Press, Seattle. 730 pp.

Franklin J. F. and C. T. Dyrness. 1973. Natural vegetation of Oregon and Washington. USDA Forest Service, Gen. Tech. Rept. PNW-8. 417 pp.

Fowells, H. A. 1965. Silvics of forest trees of the United States. USDA Forest Service, Agriculture Handbook 271. 762 pp.

Little, E. J., Jr. 1971 & 1976. Atlas of United States trees. (vols. 1 & 3, showing maps of each species' distribution). USDA Forest Service, Misc. Publ. 1146 and 1314.

Sudworth, G. B. 1908. Forest trees of the Pacific Slope. USDA Forest Service. (A classic, recently reprinted in paperback by Dover Publ. Co.) 441 pp.

Contents

Northwest Trees

Key for Identifying Northwest Trees

1a Leaves needle-like or scale-like (conifers)
. . . . .see step 2
1b Leaves not needle-like or scale-like
(broadleaved trees) . . . . .see step 23
   2a Leaves needle-like (more than ½″
      long) . . . . .see step 3
   2b Leaves scaly, tiny, pressed against
      twigs
      . . . . .see step 19
3a Needles evergreen, relatively hard or
tough
. . . . .see step 5

3b

3b Needles deciduous, dropping from tree
each fall, soft and borne mostly in small
dense clusters (larch) . . . . .see step 4
   4a The current year's twigs (tips of
      branches) covered with woolly hairs;
      tree growing near timberline
      . . . . .alpine larch, p. 47
   4b Current-year twigs with few or no
      hairs, shiny; straight, slender, tall
      tree in forests, usually far below
      timberline . . . . . . .western larch, p. 41

5a

5a Needles attached in "bundles" of 2, 3, or 5
(pine) . . . . .see step 6
5b Needles attached singly to the twigs
. . . . .see step 10
   6a Needles 2 to a bundle; about 2″ long;
      cones 1½-2″ long
      . . . . . .lodgepole and shore pine, p. 35
   6b Needles mostly more than 2 to a

6a

bundle; cones more than 2½" long
.... see step 7

7a

7a   Needles mostly in bundles of 3, 5-8" long;
cones 3-5" long .....ponderosa pine, p. 29
7b   Needles mostly in bundles of 5, 1½-4" long
.... see step 8

8a   Needles 1½-3" long, yellowish-green,
stout and rigid; cones about 3" long,
seldom found whole on the ground;
tree of high elevations, especially
near timberline
.... whitebark pine, p. 23
8b   Needles 2-4" long, bluish-green and
slender; cones at least 6" long, usually
conspicuous on the ground; large
forest trees .... see step 9

9a

9a   Cones 6-10" long (not including the stalk);
needles flexible; bark not flaky, on large
trees divided by fissures into small nearly
square blocks; tree widespread in the
Pacific Northwest
.... western white pine, p. 13
9b   Cones 10-16" long (without the stalk);
needles rather stiff and sharply pointed;
bark flaky and irregularly fissured; tree
ranging north only to the northern
Oregon Cascades
.... sugar pine, p. 19

10a

10a   Twigs of the current year remain
green; needles flat and tipped with a
slender point; fruit small, red and
berry-like; bark purplish and
shredding in papery scales; often a
low, spreading tree
.... Pacific yew, p. 136
10b   Twigs of the current year turning
brown; needles not as above; fruit a
woody cone; potentially tall forest tree
.... see step 11

11a

11a   Cones 2-4" long with three-pronged
(fork-like) bracts sticking out from
between the scales; buds sharp-pointed;
needles pointed but not prickly to the
touch .... Douglas-fir, p. 67

11b Cones without three-pronged bracts; buds
not sharp-pointed; needles often either
blunt or prickly .... see step 12

    12a Young branches smooth after needles
have fallen; needles fall off at the base
leaving round scars; cones sit erect in
the uppermost branches, but
disintegrate; thus old, whole cones
cannot be found (true firs)

        .... see step 16

    12b Young branches are rough or warty
where the needles have been shed;
needles fall leaving a small woody
base; cones not erect and not usually
confined to the uppermost branches,
remaining intact on the ground

        .... see step 13

13a Needles stiff and prickly to the touch,
giving off a strong odor when crushed;
bark with loose surface scales (spruce)

    .... see step 14

13b Needles blunt, not giving off a strong
odor; bark rough but without loose surface
scales (hemlock) .... see step 15

    14a Coastal tree found west of the
Cascade Crest and below 1500′
elevation; needles flattened, whitish
on one side; cones mostly 2½-4″ long

        .... Sitka spruce, p. 53

    14b Tree of inland mountains, along and
east of Cascade Crest, usually above
2000′ elevation; needles stout, not
flattened, similarly colored on all
sides; cones mostly 1½-2″ long

        .... Engelmann spruce, p. 60

15a Needles flat, spreading horizontally from
opposite sides of the twig to form flat
spray-like branches; cones ½-1″ long; tip
of younger trees drooping distinctly

    .... western hemlock, p. 75

15b Needles rather plump (not flat), speading
from all around small twigs or mostly
turned up (not forming flat sprays); cones

15a

15b

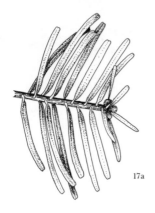

17a

17b

18a

18b

mostly 1¼-2½″ long; tip of younger trees
erect . . . . .mountain hemlock, p. 80

16a Needles flat, many or all of them
spreading horizontally from opposite
sides of the twig; branches flattened
(spray-like); needles (and thus
branches) with white bands
underneath, glossy deep green above
. . . . .see step 17

16b Needles rather plump and spreading
out like a brush at least on the upper
side of branches; needles with whitish
bands on both surfaces, thus top and
bottom of branches do not contrast
strongly in color
. . . . .see step 18

17a Needles generally 1¼-2″ long, 2-ranked
and nearly all spreading horizontally,
leaving upper side of twigs bare; tree of
low elevations when in or west of the
Cascades . . . . .grand fir, p. 92

17b Some needles (about 1″ long) spread
horizontally, but others (shorter) point
forward, covering the upper side of twigs;
tree of middle and high elevations, not
occurring east of the Cascade Mountain
System . . . . .Pacific silver fir, p. 86

18a Needles stiff and turning upward
(leaving the lower side of twigs bare);
needles with 2 whitish bands on
upper side (as well as 2 bands
underneath); bark flaking off in
scales; large tree not having a narrow
spire-like form; growing at middle
elevations in or west of the Cascades
southward from Stevens Pass (east of
Seattle) . . . . noble fir, p. 106

18b Twigs imperfectly brush-like; needles
with one broad whitish band on
upper side (in addition to 2 bands
underneath); bark not flaking off in
scales; a smaller tree with a narrow
spire-like form; abundant at high
elevations in the Pacific Northwest,

forming timberline
.... subalpine fir, p. 98

19a Branches rather bushy, not flattened and
spray-like; bears lumpy bluish berry-like
fruits about the size of a pea; small, often
shrubby trees on dry sites near northern
Puget Sound or east of the Cascades
(juniper) ....see step 20

19b Branches flattened and spray-like;
bearing small woody cones; potentially
large forest trees on moist sites
..........................see step 21

20a The tiny scale-like leaves arranged
opposite each other in pairs on the
twigs; fruits slightly under ¼" long
.... Rocky Mountain juniper, p. 130

20b The tiny scale-like leaves arranged in
whorls of 3 on the twigs; fruits slightly
over ¼" long; growing southward
from southern Washington
..............western juniper, p. 130

20a   20b

21a Cones about 1" long, appearing to be made
up of 3 large scales; the longer scale-like
leaves extend ¼-½" along the surface of
the twigs; at least the upper branches
upturned and the tree tip erect; growing
northward in the Cascades only to Mount
Hood ....incense-cedar, p. 111

21b Cones ¼-½" long, made up of several
scales; leaves generally extending less
than ¼" along twigs; upper branches
and tip at least somewhat drooping; trees
widespread in the Pacific Northwest
..........................see step 22

21a

22a Cones round; foliage droops strongly
(weeping); bark ashy gray and
flaking; leaves distinctly malodorous
when crushed; found at higher
elevations ....Alaska-cedar, p. 124

22b Cones elongated (oblong); foliage
only somewhat drooping; bark
brownish and shredding in long
fibrous strips; leaves not malodorous;
tree abundant at lower elevations
............western redcedar, p. 117

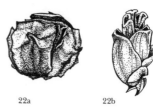

22a   22b

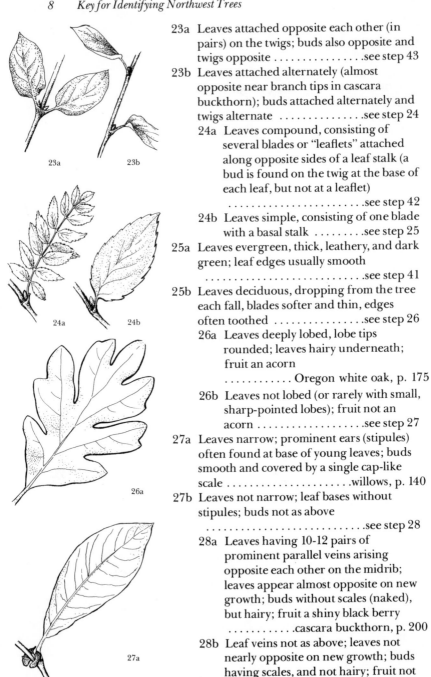

23a Leaves attached opposite each other (in pairs) on the twigs; buds also opposite and twigs opposite .... see step 43

23b Leaves attached alternately (almost opposite near branch tips in cascara buckthorn); buds attached alternately and twigs alternate .... see step 24

24a Leaves compound, consisting of several blades or "leaflets" attached along opposite sides of a leaf stalk (a bud is found on the twig at the base of each leaf, but not at a leaflet) .... see step 42

24b Leaves simple, consisting of one blade with a basal stalk .... see step 25

25a Leaves evergreen, thick, leathery, and dark green; leaf edges usually smooth .... see step 41

25b Leaves deciduous, dropping from the tree each fall, blades softer and thin, edges often toothed .... see step 26

26a Leaves deeply lobed, lobe tips rounded; leaves hairy underneath; fruit an acorn .... Oregon white oak, p. 175

26b Leaves not lobed (or rarely with small, sharp-pointed lobes); fruit not an acorn .... see step 27

27a Leaves narrow; prominent ears (stipules) often found at base of young leaves; buds smooth and covered by a single cap-like scale .... willows, p. 140

27b Leaves not narrow; leaf bases without stipules; buds not as above .... see step 28

28a Leaves having 10-12 pairs of prominent parallel veins arising opposite each other on the midrib; leaves appear almost opposite on new growth; buds without scales (naked), but hairy; fruit a shiny black berry .... cascara buckthorn, p. 200

28b Leaf veins not as above; leaves not nearly opposite on new growth; buds having scales, and not hairy; fruit not a black berry .... see step 29

29a Leaf stalks obviously flattened (test by
     rolling them between fingers), causing
     foliage to flutter noisily in a slight breeze;
     leaves nearly circular except for the
     pointed tip; bark smooth and almost white
     . . . . .quaking aspen, p. 151
29b Leaf stalks not flattened; foliage not
     fluttering in a slight breeze; leaves not
     circular; bark not *both* smooth and
     nearly white . . . . .see step 30
    30a Leaf blades generally 3-6″ long, broad
         at the base and pointed at the tip;
         buds large (¾″ long) sharp-pointed,
         sticky, and filled with fragrant red
         resin; trees becoming very large,
         developing thick, heavily furrowed
         gray bark
         . . . . black cottonwood, p. 146
    30b Leaf blades not as above; buds
         smaller and not as above; small or
         medium sized trees without heavily
         furrowed bark . . . . .see step 31
31a Small clusters of woody cone-like fruits
     (catkins) ½-¾″ long persisting on the trees
     all year; buds prominent (⅓-½″ long) and
     (except in Sitka alder) borne on a short
     stalk (alder) . . . . .see step 38
31b Trees without woody cone-like fruits; buds
     without a stalk and often small and
     inconspicuous . . . . .see step 32
    32a Fruit a narrow papery cylinder that
         disintegrates at maturity; twigs very
         slender; either the twigs are covered
         with wart-like spots (glands), or the
         tree's bark is almost white and peels
         off in papery shreds (birch)
         . . . . .see step 37
    32b Fruit berry-like; twigs and bark not
         as above . . . . .see step 33
33a Twigs with thorns or sharp spur shoots;
     leaves with coarse teeth (sometimes
     forming small lobes); fruit like a miniature
     apple . . . . .see step 36
33b Twigs without sharp projections; leaves

28a

29a

30a

31a

32a

34a

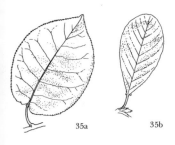

35a   35b

36a

37b

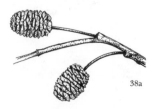

38a

having only fine teeth; fruit cherry-like
. . . . .see step 34

34a Leaves egg-shaped and pointed,
     often having a lopsided base; 3 main
     veins arise from leaf base, and vein
     network is prominent on the
     underside; leaf surfaces feel rough;
     fruit borne singly at the base of a leaf
     . . . . .netleaf hackberry, p. 188

34b Leaves not lopsided at base; veins not
     as above; leaf surfaces not rough;
     fruit borne in clusters . . . . .see step 35

35a Leaves sharp-pointed; a pair of knob-like
     glands attached to the leaf-stalk just below
     the blade; flowers and cherries in
     cylindrical clusters about 4″ long
     . . . . .western chokecherry, p. 182

35b Leaves with blunt tips; a pair of knob-like
     glands found on the base on the leaf blade;
     flowers and cherries in small rounded
     clusters (1½-2″ long)
     .bitter cherry, p. 181

36a Twigs with stout thorns ½-1″ long;
     fruit blue-black
     . . . . .black hawthorne, p. 187

36b Twigs with rough-textured, sharp
     spur shoots; fruit turning from green
     to yellow to reddish
     . . . . .Pacific crab apple, p. 185

37a Twigs covered with wart-like spots
     (glands); bark dark coppery brown, not
     peeling in papery shreds; leaf blades less
     than 2″ long, tips not sharp-pointed
     . . . . .water birch, p. 165

37b Twigs smooth; bark usually whitish and
     peeling in papery shreds; leaf blades 2-3″
     long; and sharp-pointed
     . . . . .paper birch, p. 165

38a A tall shrub of high-mountain forests,
     often growing in dense patches in
     snowslide areas; buds sharp-pointed
     and without a stalk; cone stalks as
     long as or longer than the woody
     cones . . . . .Sitka alder, p. 161

38b Usually small to medium-sized trees
growing at lower elevations; buds
generally blunt and on a short stalk;
cone stalks generally shorter than the
woody cones . . . . .see step 39

39a Abundant medium-sized tree found west
of the Cascade Crest and at low elevations
in northern Idaho; leaves with rounded
teeth, rusty tinged on the underside; leaf
edges crimped under
. . . . .red alder, p. 157

39a

39b Small trees along watercourses mostly east
of the Cascade Crest; leaves with sharp
teeth; not rusty tinged and edges not
crimped under . . . . .see step 40

  40a Leaves with large (coarse) as well as
fine teeth; leaf tips pointed
. . . . .thinleaf alder, p. 163

  40b Leaves with fine teeth only; leaf tips
rounded . . . . .white alder, p. 163

41a Leaves rounded at both base and tip; bark
flaking off in curly, ragged scales; fruit a
red berry; common tree in lowlands west
of the Cascades
. . . . .Pacific madrone, p. 209

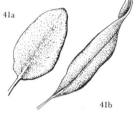

41a

41b

41b Leaves pointed at both base and tip; bark
not as above; fruit a large spiny bur; tree
common only south of Salem, Oregon
. . . . .golden chinkapin, p. 171

  42a Branches armed with pairs of thorns
at leaf bases; flower like that of a pea;
fruit a legume; leaflets with smooth
edges . . . . .black locust, p. 218

  42b Branches without thorns; flower not
pea-like; fruit berry-like; leaflets with
toothed edges
. . . . .mountain-ash, p. 218

43a Leaves compound, consisting of several
blades or "leaflets" attached along opposite
sides of a leaf stalk (a bud is found on the
twig at the base of each leaf, but not at
a leaflet) . . . . .Oregon ash, p. 214

43b Leaves simple, consisting of one blade,
which may be lobed . . . . .see step 44

44b

45a

46a

46b

44a Leaves lobed and maple-like; fruit with large wings; trees without large cream-colored blossoms (maples) ....see step 45

44b Leaves not lobed; fruit without wings; trees with large cream-colored blossoms ...... Pacific dogwood, p. 205

45a The larger leaves well over 6″ across; flowers in long hanging clusters; a large tree of low elevations from the Cascades westward .... bigleaf maple, p. 190

45b Leaves less than 6″ across; flowers in small clusters; small, often shrubby trees .... see step 46

46a Leaves with 3 to 5 lobes; small twigs often bright red; wings on the fruit bent out almost in a horseshoe; tree trunks grow erect .... Douglas maple, p. 196

46b Leaves with 7 to 9 lobes; small twigs not bright red; wings on fruit projecting in opposite directions; tree trunks often sprawling almost horizontally .... vine maple, p. 196

Western White Pine

Pinus monticola
Pine family *(Pinaceae)*

Western white pine's long, clear trunk and slender crown contrast with the dense, heavy boughs of its principal associates in the Northwest forests. Although western white pine is widely distributed throughout, strangely it is seldom more than a minor component, making up less than five percent of the trees in most stands. It can be found virtually anywhere between sea level and about 5000 feet elevation in southwestern British Columbia and in the Puget Sound or Olympic Peninsula areas. Southward in western Washington and in Oregon, and on the east slope of the Cascades, it commonly grows at elevations between 2000 and 6000 feet. Still farther south in the mountains of central California, it finds suitably cool and moist growing conditions only at about 7500 to 10,500 feet elevation.

Mature western white pines commonly grow 3 or 4 feet thick and tower 150 to 200 feet above the forest floor, but they are not really large trees by Northwest standards, and Northwesterners may not appreciate what a famous lineage this species represents. Its very similar relative, known as eastern white pine *(Pinus strobus)*, was the only softwood timber tree considered to be commercially valuable by the colonists and other early settlers in the northeastern United States. The English monarchy even blazed certain prime specimens with a broad arrow to reserve them for masts for the Royal Navy. "White pine" lured early lumbermen across the north woods from New England to Minnesota and thence to northern Idaho, where it was learned that our species, western white pine, grew in abundance and attained even larger size than its eastern kin. These early loggers might have cleared off all the primeval white pine forest here,

too, except that the era of conservation — in which Teddy Roosevelt and Gifford Pinchot figured prominently — intervened and great protective forest reserves were established.

Although western white pine is less abundant west of Idaho, it attains its largest size in the coastal Northwest forests. The largest known western white pine stands 6½ feet thick and 239 feet tall in the mountains near Medford, Oregon.

Surprisingly, white pine becomes really abundant in the coastal Northwest only on poor sites, where it can compete successfully with Douglas-fir and other conifers for growing room. In fact it outgrows other species on poor sites. On the least productive gravelly soils in the Puget Sound area, white pine makes up as much as half of the timber and reaches diameters of 3 feet, while Douglas-firs of similar age attain diameters of only 1-1½ feet. These poor sites are ideal for producing Douglas-fir Christmas trees, but the white pine grows too rapidly for that purpose. Its regularly spaced whorls (clusters) of branches, representing one year's growth, are usually more than a foot apart even on poor sites. (If a person is interested in learning the age of a white pine he can simply count the whorls of branches along the smooth young trunk and add about two years to allow for initial establishment of the seedling.) Western white pine also thrives at the edges of bogs on the Olympic Peninsula.

Young white pines are easily recognized by their narrow, open crowns made up of regularly spaced branches. Moreover, large cones dangle from the branch tips of even the young trees 15 years of age. These slender, pitchy cones, 6-10 inches long, also lie about the forest floor, making it obvious to the passerby that there is a white pine in the vicinity. In a dense old-growth forest where all the boughs are so high overhead as to make the foliage and cones indistinguishable, still another means is available for identifying western white pine: the dark-colored bark on mature trees is "checkered" or deeply cut into small, regular squares, unlike any other Northwestern tree.

Bundles (fascicles) of old needles can also be found on the ground; each bundle contains 5 slender, flexible needles. The living foliage has a distinctive whitish-blue appearance. These needle characteristics are helpful for distinguishing young western white pines at high elevations where they occasionally mingle with scattered whitebark pines at that species' lower limits. By

Western white pine

contrast, whitebark pine needles are yellowish-green, stout, and stiff.

Still another notable feature of western white pine is the way the uppermost boughs of large trees stretch out and up like arms reaching into the sky. Large cones often dangle from these lofty boughs. The cones are narrow, bright green, and heavy when tree squirrels cut them, and they crash to the ground. Western white pine seeds are comparatively small (27,000 per pound) but are a favorite of the squirrels, and squirrel caches are a favorite place for foresters to collect white pine seed for raising nursery stock.

Two seeds rest in pockets at the base of each cone scale, and most trees bear a few cones each year. In sharp contrast to many other conifers that yield hundreds or even thousands of cones per tree in a good year, 40 cones in a single tree is considered a good crop by white pine standards.

The long, clear trunk of a mature white pine contains some of the most valuable wood in the Pacific Northwest. (It has been said of the eastern white pine that no other wood known to man has been more valuable.) Western white pine wood is light in color and weight, but comparatively strong. Its grain is often so straight and even that the wood can be sliced across the grain with ease. It takes nails without splitting, works well, and takes a finish of varnish or paint nicely. It has historically been used for window and door frames and moldings, and among other uses, it is the prime material for wooden matches and toothpicks. Western white pine is outstanding for wood carving. A favorite whittler's project is to take a block of this wood and fashion it into a chain composed of many interlocking links.

Unfortunately, there is all too much standing dead western white pine, suitable mainly for whittling stock, in the forest these days. White pine timber is being depleted rapidly as a result of a fungus which man accidentally imported. Ironically, white pine blister rust *(Cronartium ribicola)* was introduced in the early 1900s when a shipment of infected white pine seedlings which had been raised in France, where labor was cheaper, arrived at a West Coast port. Blister rust is deadly to white pine in the same sense that chestnut blight, Dutch elm disease, and the gypsy moth are deadly to certain eastern hardwoods. In each case, modern man has unwittingly upset the ecological applecart by importing a foreign tree pest against which our trees have developed no natural resistance.

When blister rust spread into the stronghold of white pine in northern Idaho in the 1930s, a multimillion dollar program was launched by the federal government to save the trees. During three decades that followed, thousands of men were employed to grub out currant and gooseberry bushes (genus *Ribes*) all the way from British Columbia to northern California. By thus destroying the alternate host necessary for completion of the blister rust's life cycle, foresters hoped to save western white pine and sugar pine.

However, the rust spores can be carried by wind 10 or more miles to infect new trees, provided moisture is adequate. The *Ribes* eradication program proved nearly futile, as did a later chemical attack on the rust. Now efforts are largely concentrated upon crossbreeding the few naturally resistant white pines in order to obtain large quantities of rust-resistant stock for planting. This program is promising, largely because it seeks to enhance and speed up nature's own approach — the slow, evolutionary process of building up a resistant strain, generation by generation.

Sugar Pine

Pinus lambertiana
Pine family *(Pinaceae)*

Sugar pine is the tallest, largest, and by most accounts the most magnificent of all the world's over 100 species of pines. Its great reddish-brown trunks and towering crowns, made up of long limbs that stand out at right angles, dominate millions of acres of mountain forest in California and southwestern Oregon. It is one of only three forest trees, along with incense-cedar and golden chinkapin, that extend into the Northwest forests from the south. By contrast, 11 other species that are primarily Californian reach north only into southwestern Oregon.

Sugar pine extends north along the moist western slope of the Cascades to the headwaters of the Clackamas River 50 miles east of Salem, Oregon. It becomes increasingly common southward along the west slope of the Cascades opposite Eugene. Here it grows between elevations of 1700 and 3700 feet, but like western white pine, does not form pure stands. In northwestern Oregon it usually grows with Douglas-fir, grand fir, incense-cedar, western hemlock, western redcedar, and western white pine.

Old-growth sugar pines commonly stand 6 or 7 feet thick and 200 feet tall. The largest known living pine, in California, measures more than 10 feet thick and 216 feet in height. However, even this forest giant would be dwarfed by the sugar pine that David Douglas reported finding in 1826 in the mountains near what is now Roseburg, Oregon. (Douglas was the Scottish botanist-explorer who first described many of our Northwest trees — including Douglas-fir, which was later named for him.)

Douglas hiked off alone that rainy October in 1826, heading south from Fort Vancouver on the Columbia River, up the Willamette Valley. Local Indians watched with curiosity as he wandered through the woods collecting plant specimens, and unlike other strangers, not seeking to trade or to exploit nature's riches. They called him "Man of Grass."

Douglas had set out to find the mysterious pines with huge cones that the Indians had told him about. After walking 200 miles through essentially unexplored territory, he sighted these great pines, the largest of which he reported to be 18 feet thick and 245 feet long, which had blown over. Wanting to collect cones, he fired his gun at some hanging from the lofty branches, but the noise soon attracted eight hostile Indians.

He made futile efforts to befriend them, then resorted to cocking his gun and showing his determination to fight for his life. After several minutes of tense confrontation, the Indian leader gave a sign that they wanted tobacco. Douglas signified that he would give it to them if they fetched a quantity of the large pine cones. As soon as they walked out of sight, he grabbed his three cones and some twigs and retreated hastily from the sugar pine forest.

Sugar pine cones are mostly 10 to 16 inches long, exclusive of the heavy stalk. They dangle like Christmas ornaments from the tips of upper limbs that reach out as much as 40 feet from the massive trunk. Sugar pines do not become good cone producers until they have attained a diameter of about 30 inches or about 150 years of age; large trees often bear more than 100 cones per year. While still green, the cones weigh as much as four pounds, and since they often hang 150 feet up, it is wise to be alert when the squirrels are felling cones from sugar pine trees overhead!

Sugar pine nuts (2100 per pound) are about the size of a grain of corn and were used for food by Indians. The sugary resin, which forms crunchy crystalline deposits around a wound on the trunk, was regarded as a delicacy by the native Americans; however, when eaten in quantity, this sugar acts as a laxative. Indians used pitch from sugar pine to repair canoes and to fasten arrowheads and feathers to shafts.

Sugar pine bears 3-inch-long needles, 5 to a cluster, much like those of western white pine, but stiffer, somewhat plumper, and darker in color (bluish green). Sugar pine bark also differs from that of western white pine in being reddish brown and irregularly fissured, rather than being "checkered." The larger, stouter cones provide an additional distinction. Sugar pine, western

white pine, and whitebark are classified as "white pines," and all three are threatened by the dreaded white pine blister rust (discussed under western white pine).

Like western white pine, sugar pine is unusual among the western pines in being somewhat tolerant of shade. That is, it can reproduce successfully under a moderately heavy forest canopy — though not so successfully as the true firs and incense-cedar that accompany it. Its thick bark withstands fire, and sugar pines frequently live for 500 years.

Sugar pine wood is similar in most respects to that of eastern white pine and western white pine, but it grows on such massive trunks that it was even more appealing to the early settlers. Because of the remoteness of stands in Oregon, and the slower rate of human settlement, the impact on sugar pine was not great. However, the situation was different in nearby California: the influx of gold seekers there brought demand for house timbers, shingles, etc., and sugar pine was the answer. Giant sugar pines were plundered on thousands of acres of unprotected government land. Often only the finest wood was used, and less-than-perfect logs were left where they had been toppled. It was not until the national parks and national forests were created around the turn of the century that remnants of the once extensive forests of old growth sugar pine were granted protection.

Whitebark Pine

Pinus albicaulis
Pine family *(Pinaceae)*

Although whitebark pine is well distributed in the high mountains from central British Columbia to California and eastward to Wyoming, few auto travelers see it. In contrast, whitebark is regarded as a sort of "old friend" by many hikers and mountain climbers who frequent the high country near timberline. Whitebark commonly inhabits the upper fringe of forest, usually at or above 5500 feet elevation in southwestern British Columbia, Washington, and Oregon. It becomes abundant in the drier, inland mountains, such as on the eastern or "rain shadow" slope of the Cascades, and is restricted to the driest (northeastern) corner of the Olympic Mountains.

Roads reach the lower limits of whitebark pine in a few locations — such as Manning Provincial Park in British Columbia, at Washington Pass and Harts Pass in the North Cascades, Yakima Park on Mount Rainier, on Mount Adams, Mount Hood, and at Crater Lake. By contrast, hundreds of miles of hiking trails thread their way through rugged high-country landscape sprinkled with whitebark pines.

Because of its remote habitat, only hikers are likely to see whitebark in all the interesting growth forms by which it adapts to survival under rigorous climatic conditions. Where it extends lowest, such as down into the upper reaches of the lodgepole pine forests east of the Cascade Crest, whitebark takes on a slender, straight form remarkably like that of lodgepole pine. This is the growth form of whitebark that is occasionally logged, when it is found with other more desirable timber species. Some of the lowest known naturally occurring whitebark pines associate with western white pines on a south-facing slope below Government Camp on Mount Hood at about 3800 feet elevation.

At higher elevations, where the forest begins to break up into groves of trees and meadows, whitebark gains more living space and develops a stout, short trunk 40 to 80 feet tall, and a large, spreading crown. Trees like this provide plump blue grouse a place to roost, protected by the dense boughs from the on-slaughts of winter and from sight of marauding goshawks and human hunters. When, after several centuries, these stout trees topple, their bulky limbs supply campers with easily broken chunks of pitchy fuel for a crackling fire.

Near timberline, each whitebark pine typically develops several trunks 15 to 40 feet tall, joined only at ground level. These multi-stemmed trees often bear good cone crops, and are short enough to allow one a good view of the Clark's nutcrackers — a colorful black, white, and gray jay — noisily pounding away on the purple cones in the tree top to extract the rich nuts.

At a still higher altitude, whitebark pine becomes a huge sprawling shrub or 5- to 12-foot-tall "krummholz" — meaning literally "crooked wood" in German. Often the tallest stems develop into wind-battered "flags" because they protrude from the protective winter snow pack and are thus thrashed by ice-blasting gales. On south-facing slopes, whitebark krummholz sometimes develops into an almost impenetrable thicket, but

Krummholz

Whitebark pine

many climbers and mountain goats have been grateful for the shelter this dense growth provided during a sudden storm. Naturalist John Muir once counted annual growth-rings on some of these shrublike whitebark pines, describing one as "...426 years old, whose trunk is only six inches in diameter; and one of its supple branchlets, hardly an eighth of an inch in diameter inside the bark, is seventy-five years old, and so filled with oily balsam, and so well seasoned by storms, that we may tie it in knots like whipcord."

Finally, in the alpine tundra far above the highest trees, the hiker is likely to encounter still another form of whitebark pine. Here it becomes a little wind-pruned shrub, only 1 or 2 feet high, often huddled in the lee of a large rock. The crown of such a conifer cushion, also known as "alpine scrub," is composed of hundreds of tiny branchlets making a perfectly hedged surface. The gardener that each year shears off protruding shoots is the winter wind. Relentless blizzards blast the twigs with grains of ice and sand, and winds dry out any exposed green shoots during the time that the ground is frozen and water for transpiration is unavailable. These alpine cushions of whitebark pine can be found as high as 8000 feet in the northern Cascades, 9000 feet in Oregon, and 12,000 feet in the California Sierra Nevada.

Both the common and scientific names (*Pinus albicaulis* is literally "white-stemmed pine") denote the whitish color on the stem of young trees. However, parts of the trunk that are exposed to ice-blasting winds, such as in the krummholz zone, are polished to a rosy hue. Stouter trees develop scaly, grayish bark; they grow slowly but become 3 or even 4 feet thick by the time they are 500 to 700 years of age. East of the Cascades, many of these large patriarch-like whitebarks have been killed in mountain pine beetle epidemics, and form grotesque snags atop the lofty ridges. Unlike many insects and diseases that take their toll mostly from the smaller and weaker trees, mountain pine beetles usually kill only the larger whitebark and lodgepole pines. This phenomenon occurs because only the larger trees provide a sap layer (cambium) thick enough for the beetles to raise their larvae in. The larvae eat tunnels in the sap layer, often girdling the tree.

Whitebark is also susceptible to white pine blister rust, and many trees in the moister mountain areas, such as some of the small stands in the Olympic Mountains, have been ravaged by this introduced disease. However, in much of whitebark's range, on drier mountains, blister rust has had little effect, possibly because dry summer conditions are less favorable for its development.

Whitebark can be distinguished from western white pine and sugar pine by its stout, stiff, yellow-green needles (also in bundles of 5), and by its much smaller cones. In fact, these cones are very distinctive, since they are the only North American "pine" cones that disintegrate at maturity (like cones of a true fir) rather than opening to shed seed and then lying intact on the ground for several years.

These disintegrating cones provide the only simple clue for distinguishing whitebark from its relative, limber pine (*Pinus flexilis*), where the two species grow together eastward in the Rocky Mountains (along and east of the Continental Divide in Montana, and in eastern Idaho). Limber pine cones contrast with those of whitebark by remaining intact on the ground for several years. Also, they turn from green to light brown as they ripen, compared with the dark purple of whitebark cones. Isolated groves of limber pine west of their normal range limits can be seen along the Trans-Canada Highway east of Golden, British Columbia; this species has also been reported to be growing on limestone in the Wallowa Mountains of northeastern Oregon.

Whitebark has a closer relative in Europe — a squatty timberline tree with a disintegrating cone, well known in the Alps as stone pine *(Pinus cembra)*.

Like stone pine, whitebark provides an important food source for animals of the high country. Red squirrels and Clark's nutcrackers ascend to the tree tops in late August and September to attack the plump purple cones, 2 to 3½ inches long, which contain the nearly pea-size nuts. The raucous nutcrackers issue harsh "kr-a-a-a's!" and cleverly extract the hard-shelled seeds (2600 per pound) by hammering a hole in just one side of the thick-scaled cone.

Red squirrels rip off the cone scales to feast on the seeds, but they also fell large quantities of cones and store them in rotten logs and in the ground. Sometimes black bears, and grizzly bears in the Rocky Mountains, become involved through sniffing out and raiding the squirrels' cone caches. Chipmunks, golden-mantled ground squirrels, and deer mice dine on loose whitebark pine seeds that have fallen to the ground. They also make small seed caches in the surface soil — many of which lie forgotten until the following summer, then germinate and produce a clump of whitebark seedlings.

Red squirrel and Clark's nutcracker feeding on pine nuts

Ponderosa Pine

Pinus ponderosa
Pine family *(Pinaceae)*

Ponderosa pine, perhaps more than any other tree, seems to be associated with the unconquered spirit and wide-open spaces of the American West. This tall, stately tree forms open park-like stands on sunny mountain slopes, high plateaus, and valleys from British Columbia well into Mexico, and eastward to Nebraska.

Lewis and Clark made the first written accounts of it on their 1804-1806 journey from St. Louis to the Pacific. These explorers traveled through and camped beneath ponderosa pines along much of their route, between eastern Montana and the Columbia River Gorge. Many of the individual trees that Lewis and Clark passed are undoubtedly still standing, since ponderosas often attain ages of 400 to 500 years.

Twenty years later, the botanical explorer David Douglas named these trees "ponderosa" because of their great size. Old-growth trees average about 3 feet in diameter and 120 feet in height, and large trees are often 4 or 5 feet thick. The largest recorded ponderosa, growing along the Deschutes River south of Bend in central Oregon, is nearly 9 feet in diameter and 161 feet tall.

Scattered ponderosa pines grow in a few locations west of the Cascades — the upper Skagit Valley, near Lake Crescent, and south of Tacoma (all in Washington), and in the Willamette Valley of northwestern Oregon. By contrast, ponderosa is abundant in the drier country east of the Cascade Crest. Here it forms vast forests spreading down the skirts of the mountains and merging with the sagebrush and bunchgrass prairies on sites too dry to support even this drought-tolerant tree.

In Oregon ponderosa pine is usually able to grow in locations receiving as little as 12 inches annual precipitation and may require even less precipitation farther north. Its ability to grow on sites drier than other forest trees can tolerate has been investigated by foresters. In one study in an arid location year-old seedlings of ponderosa attained a height of only 3 inches, but astonishingly they developed taproots nearly 2 feet long. Four-year-olds averaged a foot in height but had sunk their roots 5 feet into the parched earth. Just a few tufts of leaves are supplied moisture by an extensive root system. Perhaps because of these deep roots gardeners find it difficult to successfully transplant ponderosa pine saplings. Other studies disclosed that ponderosa requires less water than other conifers to keep its foliage alive, and that ponderosa seedlings were able to withstand exceedingly high temperatures (162° F., or 72° C.) at the ground surface in July.

As one might suspect, the warm, dry summers often bring wildfires in ponderosa pine stands; historically these have been ignited by lightning or by Indians. Once it has passed through the vulnerable sapling stage, ponderosa develops thick bark that makes it highly resistant to death by fire. Large trees often have blackened wounds or "catfaces," caused by a sequence of fires, on the uphill or leeward side of their trunks. However, this species usually seals the fire scar with pitch, which prevents damaging insects and decay organisms from gaining entry.

Some of these catfaces were initiated by fires 300 to 400 years ago, and yet the trees remain healthy. One tree that was felled recently on a ridge in the Bitterroot Mountains showed unmistakable evidence that it had been scarred by 21 separate fires beween the years 1659 and 1919, but the tree remained alive and healthy. Such frequent natural fires historically kept dead limbs, snags, needle-litter, and other fuels from building up to the dangerously high levels that might cause a holocaust. In the last several years foresters have been attempting to re-establish fire, through controlled or prescribed burning, in a number of ponderosa pine forests throughout the West, with the hope of reducing heavy accumulations of fuels that have developed over several decades as a result of fire control practices. After this initial fuel reduction has been accomplished, they will use light ground fires to perpetuate a more natural (and favorable) level of fuels.

Interestingly, black bears seem to favor the charred catfaces

on ponderosa pines for their claw-sharpening exercises. Usually these bear-paw scrapes can also be seen extending up the large orange trunks. One wonders how so heavy an animal, hanging on only by its toe nails, can walk up these smooth, pillar-like boles.

Ponderosa is described as being intolerant of shade. Without fire or other disturbance to open up the stands, ponderosa is unable to regenerate and replace itself on the moister sites where it grows mixed with more shade-tolerant conifers like Douglas-fir. Ponderosa generally requires a lot of growing space; thus stands of these large orange-barked trees are typically open. The trees' extensive root systems underly the spaces in the stand, collecting water and nutrients there.

After logging or a holocaust, young stands often start out too dense and the small trees become spindly and prone to snow damage or vulnerable to insect epidemics. If they are thinned by fire, insects, or man, remaining trees that have adequate foliage will soon begin vigorous growth. This "release" of ponderosa pine has even been noted in 200-year-old trees, when increased growing room suddenly became available.

Flakes of ponderosa pine bark

Ponderosa is a major timber species in most of the West, except for the Northwest Coast, but as a timber tree one might say it has a split personality. Ponderosa or "western yellow pine" are terms that apply only to the wood of large, old-growth trees, the ones having orange, platy bark. This wood is often clear and even-grained, having many of the fine properties of wood from western white pine and sugar pine; thus it is quite valuable, and is used for window and door frames as well as for finishing work. By contrast, trees of this species that are less than about 100 or 120 years of age are known in the timber trade as "bull pine." They have the dark-colored immature bark and rather coarse, knotty wood that is of comparatively low value, except when sold as knotty pine paneling!

Ponderosa pine wood, unlike that of white pine, is not durable when in direct contact with the ground. However, the butts and taproots of large trees are often filled with pitch, perhaps as a response to past injury or beetle attacks. When these trees are cut, and especially if the stumps are charred afterwards, the stumps become so hard and pitchy that they seem virtually indestructible. Some of the pitch stumps observed in western Montana are the remains of trees logged 90 years ago; but they are still so solid that they noticeably dull a chain saw.

Ponderosa pitch stumps are a surprisingly valuable resource. They yield large quantities of pitch kindling that will start off a roaring blaze in the snowiest weather. Before modern wood preservatives became readily available, farmers split these pitchy tree butts up into "pitch posts" for long-lasting fences. Moreover, at least one timber-products company has inventoried ponderosa pitch stumps, just to be ready in case market conditions for turpentine and rosin change substantially. Evidently ponderosa pitch stumps represent a cheap and sizeable source of these materials.

Ponderosa is most abundant between elevations of 1500 and 4000 feet east of the Cascade Crest, especially in the sunny interior of southern British Columbia, Washington, and Oregon. It sometimes ascends south-facing slopes to 5000 feet or more, particularly in southern Washington and Oregon, but it reaches its upper limits at a comparatively modest elevation for a mountain conifer. Ponderosa pines found scattered on southern exposures still higher up are stunted by repeated frost damage to their growing shoots.

This species is unlikely to be confused with any other Northwest tree since it is the only one typically bearing its long needles (5"-8") in bundles of 3. The cones are also distinctively egg-shaped, 3 to 5 inches long, and armed with a sharp prickle on the back of each cone scale. In southwestern Oregon and California it is more difficult to distinguish this species because of the presence of a closely related tree known as Jeffrey pine *(Pinus jeffreyi)*. Still, Jeffrey pine cones are substantially larger and their prickles bend back (down) rather than sticking directly out like those on ponderosa cones. Also, the mature bark of Jeffrey pine is reddish-brown, not divided into the unmistakable

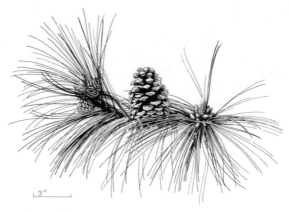

_3"_

Ponderosa pine

large orange plates of an old-growth ponderosa.

Another fascinating bark characteristic is used for telling these two species apart: foresters sniff the furrows in the bark, because those of Jeffrey pine usually have a strong vanilla-extract fragrance, while ponderosa does not. However, here in the Northwest, far beyond the northern limits of Jeffrey pine, the old-growth ponderosas occasionally smell strongly of vanilla.

Lodgepole Pine and Shore Pine

Pinus contorta
Pine family *(Pinaceae)*

This small pine can be found growing from the Yukon Territory and the Alaska Panhandle south to Baja California and east
to the Black Hills of South Dakota, but its elevational range is
even broader, since it grows from the salt spray zone on the
Pacific Coast up almost to timberline in the high mountains. This
represents a range from sea level to 8000 feet elevation in Oregon, and from sea level to nearly 11,000 feet in California!

How a single tree species could tolerate such a vast range of
environments has been pondered by many a botanist, and even
the conservative ones concede that this species is made up of at
least two varieties. The coastal form, known as shore pine, is
aptly described by the scientific name *Pinus contorta* variety *contorta* (contorted or crooked pine). The inland form, *Pinus contorta*
variety *latifolia*, was reportedly first called "lodgepole pine" by
explorers Lewis and Clark (1804-1806); they discovered that Indians from the upper Great Plains journeyed high into the Rockies to cut these straight, slender trees for poles to support their
lodges or tepees. Even today lodgepole pine is a principal source
of poles as well as posts and house logs.

Shore pine inhabits a variety of poor sites along the Pacific
Coast from Alaska to northern California. It is commonly seen
as a twisted little tree growing on soggy "muskeg" or peat bogs in
the north, on coastal sand dunes in Oregon, or even clinging to
rock cliffs. It is also widespread in the coastal lowlands of southwestern British Columbia and in the Puget Sound area, often on
either marshy or gravelly sites, where Douglas-fir and western
hemlock do not grow vigorously and thus exclude it. Where
sheltered from the coastal gales, shore pine develops a large

Shore pine

rounded crown and is limbed to the ground. Also in contrast to lodgepole pine (the inland form), shore pine's foliage is dark green, and older trees have dark-colored bark about an inch thick. Lodgepole pine usually has a narrow crown and yellow-green needles. Its bark is reddish-brown, scaly, and only about ¼ of an inch thick.

Lodgepole pine occupies vast areas in the mountains of western North America. It is abundant east of the Cascade Crest, and rather sparse on the west side. It grows with nearly all of the other mountain conifers, but often forms dense, nearly pure stands of straight, slender trees.

Central Oregon offers some difficult growing conditions for lodgepole pine: on the eastern slope of the Cascades, lodgepole grows on a thin layer of soil resting atop hardened clay. This shallow soil is almost always soggy because water cannot drain through the clay pan. Lodgepole develops a shallow rooting system and forms forests on these sites, whereas ponderosa pine is restricted to the adjacent, better drained sites. Lodgepole pine occupies frost-pockets throughout its range, and it can withstand temperatures as low as 15° F. (−9 C.) without injury during the

Lodgepole pine ▶

period when its shoots are actively growing. One researcher found that some lodgepole sites in central Oregon have frost more than half of the days during summer.

South of Puget Sound the two forms are generally separated, shore pine being confined to low-lying areas near the coast, and lodgepole found mostly above 3000 or 4000 feet in the Cascades. From Puget Sound north *most* of the *Pinus contorta* occurs either in very low-lying areas (shore pine) or high in the mountains (lodgepole pine), but small amounts of it can be found along the lower mountain slopes lying in between. In these intermediate sites it may be difficult to differentiate between the two varieties.

However, there is no difficulty in distinguishing *Pinus contorta* (shore pine and lodgepole pine) from all other Northwest trees. Only this species bears its short needles (2 inches long) in bundles of 2. Also, it has a distinctive little cone, 1½-2 inches long and covered with prickles. Campers in the high country soon learn to clear away the lodgepole pine cones before laying out their sleeping bags.

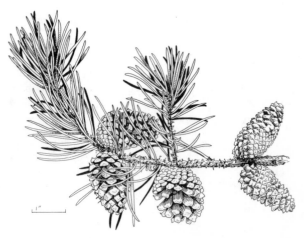

Lodgepole/shore pine

The cones and seeding habits of lodgepole have a strong relationship to other aspects of this species' ecology. In some areas many of the cones on this inland form have their scales sealed shut by resin, locking the seeds inside. This "serotinous" cone is an adaptation to intense forest fires. When such trees are burned, the heat from the fire melts the resin bond, allowing the small seeds to fall out into the ashes and newly exposed mineral soil. Thus, lodgepole pine gets a head start in burned areas, while other conifers must largely seed in from the adjacent un-burned forest or from isolated trees that survived the hot fire. In this serotiny, as well as in its general appearance, lodgepole is similar to jack pine *(Pinus banksiana)* that is so abundant in the Great Lakes States and across Canada westward to central Al-berta, where it meets and occasionally hybridizes with lodgepole.

Both lodgepole and shore pines are precocious and prolific cone-bearers, usually yielding some fruit by about 10 years of age. Often the cones hang on trees for decades; thus some trees appear loaded with thousands of burs. The seeds are so small that it takes about 100,000 to make a pound. Perhaps surpris-ingly, these tiny seeds remain viable even while being locked inside serotinous cones for many years. The closed cones some-times cling so long to small limbs near the trunk that they be-come enveloped and completely encased in wood. When lodge-pole is sawn into boards these cones are occasionally exposed; in one study the seed from a 150-year-old cone imbedded in such a board was tested and found to be viable.

But lodgepole does not have to depend upon fire or unusually hot sunshine to unlock its seeds. Even in stands having a high percentage of serotinous cones, there are usually ample amounts of unsealed cones that open and spread their seed at maturity. The net result of this copious seed supply is often what foresters call "over-stocking," an overly dense stand where the trees stag-nate because of inadequate growing space. Lodgepole pine stands eastward from the Cascade Crest to the Rockies fre-quently appear to be dense growths of saplings, when in fact they are much older trees whose growth is stunted because of over-stocking. One of these "dog-hair lodgepole stands" (where the trees grow seemingly as close as hairs on a dog's back) was found to consist of 70-year-old trees only 4 feet tall and 1 inch thick at ground level. The stand had 100,000 of these trees per acre, or an average spacing of only 8 inches between trees.

On sites where natural stocking has been more favorable, or where thinning has taken place, lodgepole produces slender trees ideal for poles, log cabins, two-by-fours, or a number of other uses. Even the sound snags, killed by fire or beetles 10 to 20 years ago, are used for these purposes. Usually this species does not live more than 150 or 200 years, among other reasons because older trees become increasingly susceptible to attack by mountain pine beetle, and often their vigor is sapped by the parasitic plant known as dwarfmistletoe *(Arceuthobium americanum)*.

Dwarfmistletoe is similar to the Christmas mistletoe except that it has only tiny scale-like leaves. Although it infects most conifer species, it is especially widespread and destructive on lodgepole pine. After the sticky dwarfmistletoe seed lands on a branch it germinates and sends a root-like growth into the branch. Eventually this spreads and causes conspicuous swellings and dense bushy growths called "witches brooms" to develop on the branches.

The small, yellowish dwarfmistletoe plant can be seen growing out of the limbs, especially in summer when the fruits are maturing. These are little capsules that explode at maturity, hurling the seed several feet and thus allowing the infection to spread slowly on an annual basis. Under natural conditions wildfires apparently helped to keep this disease in check by periodically killing dwarfmistletoe over large areas, when the forest burned; it would then spread back slowly into the new stands, migrating from surrounding unburned areas.

Coastal Indians probably did not make much use of the contorted shore pine for poles, but they reportedly employed it as a medicine. They put the pitch in open sores and chewed the buds to relieve sore throats. Another native that enjoys chewing both shore pine and lodgepole pine is the ubiquitous porcupine. These creatures eat the sap layer, or cambium, on the trunks, especially in winter; the scars they leave can often be seen high in the crowns. Porcupine damage is especially extensive east of the Cascades in Oregon; one study found that a single animal may injure 100 lodgepole pines in one winter.

WELCOME ABOARD

CALGARY TRANSIT
TRANSFER CONDITIONS

This transfer is valid only on the day of issue for one trip in a single direction on the first connecting transit vehicle within 90 minutes of the time indicated hereon. IT DOES NOT GIVE THE HOLDER THE RIGHT TO STOP OVER.

It is forbidden to sell, exchange or reproduce a transfer.

This transfer must be carried as proof of payment on the C-Train and within fare restricted areas. It must be shown to an authorized officer of the City of Calgary or to a Peace Officer upon request. Failure to present proof of payment is an offence subject to a penalty.

In case of a misunderstanding, please pay fare and report the facts to the Calgary Transit Office.

**GENERAL MANAGER,
CALGARY TRANSIT**

Transit Information
Phone 276-7801

500	45
600	30
700	15
800	50
900	45
1000	30
1100	15
1200	50
1300	45
1400	30
1500	15
1600	50
1700	45

Sp	EM	N	E	W	S	os
1 2 3 4 5 6 7 8 9 0						
1 2 3 4 5 6 7 8 9 0						
1 2 3 4 5 6 7 8 9 0						

Western Larch

Larix occidentalis
Pine family *(Pinaceae)*

Western larch is the large "evergreen" tree that surprises so many forest visitors in autumn by turning color and dropping all its needles. This is confusing to many Westerners because all the other needle-leaved trees (conifers) that they have seen remain green the year around. Western larch, however, is one of about 10 species of larch *(Larix)* that occupy many of the cooler regions of the Northern Hemisphere, and all of them are deciduous needle-leaved trees. The only other deciduous conifers native to North America are the baldcypresses *(Taxodium* spp.) of the Southeast.

People who are familiar with forests of the northeastern United States and Canada often identify western larch at first sight as a "tamarack," because of its obvious similarity to the tamarack or eastern larch *(Larix laricina)* found in those regions. However, tamarack is a relatively small tree that usually grows on boggy ground, while western larch becomes quite large and is a major constituent of the mountain forests. The third species of larch in North America, like western larch, also grows in the inland Northwest, but it is restricted to the highest peaks, near timberline. It is alpine larch *(Larix lyallii)*, the subject of our next chapter.

Western larch grows on north-facing slopes and other moderately moist sites east of the Cascade Crest in northern Oregon, Washington, and southern British Columbia, and extends eastward to northern Idaho and western Montana. In British Columbia and Washington it grows mostly between elevations of 2000 and 5500 feet, while it occurs mostly between 3000 and 7000 feet in Oregon. Western larch is abundant in the forested areas of southeastern British Columbia, northeastern Washington, and northeastern Oregon, but its occurrence on the east slope of the Cascades is more spotty. Fine stands can be seen on the highways immediately east of White Pass and Chinook Pass in Washington, and one stand is visible on a north-facing slope south of Interstate 90 a few miles west of Cle Elum. It can easily be seen growing along the eastern portion of the Mount Hood Loop Road and (farther south) from Wapinitia Pass to Bear Springs in the Oregon Cascades.

Western larch can be identified readily by its soft, light-green needles (in summer) that grow mostly in clusters on small woody lumps, or spur shoots. In October the needles turn yellowish, and by the end of that month they are brilliant golden-yellow, enabling an observer at a vantage point to spot all the western larch for miles around. From November through mid-April the larch are also conspicuous, since they stand straight and tall but without foliage. Larch limbs are readily identifiable by their lumpy appearance, created by woody spur shoots. The cones are rather papery, about 1-1½ inches long, and have small, pointed bracts sticking out from between each scale.

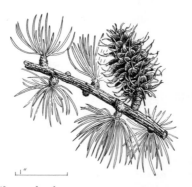

Western larch

Western larch's fall coloration is especially impressive because this tree, the largest of the world's larches, is usually as tall or taller than any of its associates. Old-growth western larch are commonly 3 or 4 feet thick and tower 150 feet above the forest floor. Exceptionally tall larch in the inland forests reach 180 to 200 feet in height. The reddish, pillar-like trunks of large trees stretch 50 feet or more to the lowermost limb. Larch is said to have a larger proportion of clear trunk, compared with its total

Ramona
Hammerly

height, than any other American trees except for the California redwoods and sequoias.

The very bases of larch trees appear fluted largely because at ground level the bark becomes astonishingly thick. This dense reddish bark, often 6 inches thick on old-growth trees, and 3 or 4 inches at the foot of second-growth trees, serves as splendid insulation, protecting the trees from injury in all but the most intense forest fires; western larch is considered the most fire-resistant of all the northwestern trees.

Western larch forms extensive mixed stands with lodgepole pine on many sites that have been burned by rather intense lightning fires. While such fires generally kill lodgepole pine, its closed cones survive and release seed for the new forest. Larch seed for regenerating the burned forest is provided by the many old-growth larch trees that usually survive even an intense conflagration. Larch seeds are light (143,000 per pound) and have a large wing, allowing great numbers of them to be carried 400 feet or more from the parent tree.

Western larch and lodgepole pine, in that order, are the fastest growing young trees on many sites in the inland Northwest, thus they can quickly capitalize on the newly available growing space after a fire. Western larch may reach 4 feet in height at 4 years of age, while Douglas-fir on the same site is only about half as tall. This rapid initial growth is essential for western larch since it is extremely intolerant of shade; it must be the tallest tree in the new stand or it will not be able to compete with its evergreen associates, and they will soon shade it out.

Once western larch is well established it can easily last through the interval until another fire occurs, since it commonly lives 500 years or more. (Western larch trees 900 years of age have been found in western Montana.) Thus, after a century or so, the rapid growth is gradually succeeded by enduring, slower growth. The resulting close annual rings make the wood of mature trees exceedingly dense. The butt logs have such large quantities of a gum stored in them that sometimes they will not even float.

Western larch wood is the densest (heaviest) of any Northwest conifer, and is also quite durable. The wood of large snags that were killed in fires 50 to 70 years ago is harvested and made into shakes. It has a high heating value and splits readily, yielding one of the finest fuel woods available in the Northwest. Larch is used commercially for poles and cut into construction lumber and flooring.

Giant sun-bleached larch snags characteristically tower above many a young forest east of the Cascade Crest. These often attract lightning strikes and then serve as kindling for a forest fire. A hot crown fire is likely to be responsible for conversion of the living larch into a snag in the first place, but other factors may have contributed also. Dwarfmistletoe infects western larch much as it does lodgepole pine, and after perhaps a century or more of supporting this disease, an old-growth larch will often retain only a few clubby branches.

Another factor in the natural death of western larch is a large whitish fungus called quinine conk *(Fomes officinalis)*, often visible high up on the trunk. One of these conks, or bracket fungi, indicates to a forester that the tree is so rotten as to be worthless for timber. Such a conk is the fruiting body for an extensive network of fungus inside the tree; but quinine conk is particularly interesting because for many years it was harvested (by shooting it off with a rifle) and sold by the pound to pharmaceutical manufacturers in Europe, to whom it had medicinal value. The fungus inside the trunk is equally interesting, because it forms a uniform layer of white felt-like material, known as "mycelial felt."

These rotting larch trees are of considerable value to forest animals. Cavities in the great trunks make homes for flying squirrels, woodpeckers, owls, and many species of songbirds. Ospreys, bald eagles, and even Canada geese occasionally make their large platform-like nests on these snags. The succulent larch needles have been found to be a major food source for both blue grouse and spruce or Franklin grouse.

A serious threat to the continued productivity of western larch stands became apparent in 1957, when foresters in northern Idaho discovered the beginnings of an outbreak of small insects known as larch casebearer *(Coleophora laricella)*. This species is a native of Europe that was accidentally imported to the eastern United States in the late 1800s. It eats the new needles of larches in Europe and eastern North America, but its populations there are kept in check by many species of parasites. However, casebearer has now repeatedly defoliated western larch trees over large areas of the inland Northwest, and attempts to control it through the introduction of parasites have had little success so far.

Being deciduous, larch trees resist defoliation caused by insects or diseases better than other conifers, which have more difficulty replacing the lost foliage. The larch produces a second crop of needles in late spring when the first crop has been largely devoured. Still, repeated defoliation slows tree growth dramatically, and may prevent western larch from continuing to compete successfully with other trees in the forest.

Alpine Larch

Larix lyallii
Pine family *(Pinaceae)*

Only a small percentage of outdoorsmen in the Pacific Northwest has ever walked through a grove of alpine larch, but those that have are likely to remember it. This tree commonly grows in small, open stands so high up on the mountainsides that its only associates are shrub-like growths of subalpine fir or whitebark pine. Alpine larch trees have open crowns covered with soft, light-green needles that turn golden-yellow in early autumn before dropping from the tree.

Alpine larch is a deciduous conifer that often forms park-like stands at or above the limits of the evergreen conifers. This remarkable hardiness was perhaps first described in detail in the late 1890s by two naturalists who were sent out to explore the largely untracked wilderness that had recently been placed into "forest reserves," forerunners of today's national forests. Naturalist Henry Ayres returned from the remote mountains of the inland Northwest and reported finding this larch to be "a sturdy alpine tree resisting the snows and snowslides better than any other species." He had also found that the largest alpine larch grow "about the heads of basins where snow lingers late into summer or in banks entirely through the season."

Another of these early investigators, John Leiberg, reported that this tree above all others, "is fashioned to withstand successfully the rigorous climatic conditions prevailing on the high and bleak summits." Leiberg also offered the following explanation of this tree's astonishing hardiness:

> "With a light and graceful foliage, offering slight resistance to the winter's blasts, a compact, strong trunk and a root system firmly anchored in the crevices of the underlying rocks, it can bid defiance to winds of any violence, and it is very rarely, indeed that one sees an individual of this species uprooted."

Alpine larch

Alpine larch grows only in the highest mountain ranges of the inland Northwest. It occurs along a north-south distance of about 120 miles in the Cascades, compared to nearly 430 miles in the Northern Rockies. It occupies the high ranges east of the Cascade Crest from the latitude of Wenatchee, Washington, northward across the border a few miles into British Columbia, in Manning Provincial Park and the Ashnola River drainage. A few roads lead into the lower reaches of alpine larch — including the North Cascades Highway, where scattered trees can be seen in the rockpiles at the foot of north-facing mountainsides near 5250-foot Washington Pass. The road to Harts Pass (6200 feet) farther north on the Cascade Divide leads into stands of alpine larch mixed with subalpine fir, whitebark pine, Engelmann spruce, and mountain meadows. In Manning Park, British Columbia, a road leads to a small, isolated grove of this species on the north side of Blackwall Peak. However, to really appreciate this interesting tree in its many life-forms and beautiful settings, one must still set out afoot like those early naturalists. Hiking routes that go beyond the 6000-foot level in the Stuart, Chiwaukum, Chelan, Sawtooth, and Okanogan Ranges, as well as the North Cascades proper (east of the divide) head into alpine larch country.

East from the Okanogan Range there lies a gap of 125 air miles in the distribution of alpine larch — the nearest stands in

the Rocky Mountain System being found in the Selkirk Range of southeastern British Columbia and northern Idaho. The apparent reason for this gap is a lack of adequately high mountains. This species has not been found growing below 5000 feet elevation even in the deep-snow country of the Cascade Crest, and it does poorly in cultivation, suggesting that it may require the cold summers of high mountain sites.

Farther east, alpine larch becomes abundant atop the Purcell Mountains and the Rockies in southeastern British Columbia as well as from Banff National Park in neighboring Alberta southward through western Montana. Still, throughout its range in the Rockies, alpine larch cannot be reached on a paved road.

Because of its lofty habitat, it is unlikely that this species would be confused with its relative western larch *(Larix occidentalis)*; but occasionally it extends downward in boulder piles or avalanche chutes to the uppermost limits of western larch. Even in these rare cases where they grow together the differences between the two species are distinctive. The new twigs of alpine larch are covered with woolly hairs, while those of western larch appear to be essentially smooth. Even ancient trees of alpine larch have thin bark (about an inch thick), while basal bark on western larch is several inches thick. Alpine larch has long, spreading limbs, forming a broad crown, while western larch grows much taller and with a narrow crown. Even when growing side by side, alpine larch turns color (late September) and drops its needles a month earlier than western larch.

Understandably, some biologists have concluded that alpine larch is a curious little tree; actually it is neither strange nor small. All but one of the world's 10 larch species grow at timberline either in the high mountains or in the Arctic tundra — the exception is western larch. Larches similar in many respects to our alpine larch form timberline in the European Alps, the Himalayas (as high up as 15,000 feet elevation), and in Siberia (where they extend to a latitude 120 miles farther north than that of Point Barrow, Alaska). In terms of size, alpine larch is often quite large for a timberline dweller. Trees on sheltered slopes, particularly those growing in rock piles at the head of basins, frequently reach 3 feet in diameter and 70 to 80 feet in height at maturity (typically 500 to 700 years). The largest known alpine larch grows in a steep, rocky basin at 6200 feet elevation above Lake Chelan; it is 6¼ feet thick and 94 feet tall,

with a great, spreading crown. Interestingly, this tree is characteristic of very old alpine larch in having only a thin outer shell
of sound wood, and a vast, hollow (rotted-out) interior; the
dense wood is so strong that the trunk can endure hurricane-
force winds for centuries despite massive heart-rot.

Although alpine larch has adapted to eking out an existence
on sites that are either too cold, too rocky, too boggy, or too
snow-covered for other trees, it is very intolerant of shade, and
cannot compete with evergreen conifers on more favorable sites.
Alpine larch is what is known as a "pioneer" species, meaning
that it can colonize sites that have not previously been occupied
by any vegetation. Thus it is commonly the first tree to grow on
moraines at the foot of active glaciers, and on fresh boulder piles
where even lichens and other tiny rock-dwelling plants are just
beginning to get established.

After centuries of weathering and rudimentary soil forma-
tion, other trees come in beneath the larch. Often subalpine fir,
whitebark pine, or Engelmann spruce can be seen growing up
through the sheltering crown of a veteran larch, using it as a
trellis for support against the battering gales; a single, large
larch may become a "patriarch" sheltering a cluster of smaller
evergreens whose tallest trunks will be broken off when the larch
finally topples in old age. One such larch (38 inches thick and 50
feet tall) growing on a rocky outcrop at Park Creek Pass in the
North Cascades shelters a grove of 16 small subalpine firs, 24
mountain hemlocks, and a whitebark pine.

Another situation where this larch succeeds best is in snowslide and avalanche chutes. Groves of small, pole-sized larch (up
to 5 inches thick) can be flattened annually by snow-slides and
yet pop up again undamaged when the snow melts in July. As
the trees get too large to survive this flattening, some of them
snap off, but others are strong and fortunate enough to endure
until they become so stout that even a larger avalanche cannot
destroy them.

This species gets a head start on the growing season on the
highest, coldest sites by leafing out in early June despite remaining snowpack 6 or 7 feet deep that encases the trunks. For some
unknown reason, the lower branches of saplings retain their
green needles the year-around.

The purplish new cones emerge with the foliage about June
first, but severe frost destroys them afterwards during most

years. Fresh snowfalls are not unusual even in July and August. The result is that successful cone crops are rather exceptional, and even then chances for seedling survival under the harsh climatic conditions are poor. During several years of observation one researcher reported that he had been unable to find even one new alpine larch seedling. The smallest tree he discovered was 2 inches high, but proved to be 10 years old! Still, alpine larch evidently regenerates very successfully once in a great while, when seed crops and survival conditions happen to be ideal. Unlike its evergreen associates (especially subalpine fir and mountain hemlock) it seldom reproduces vegetatively, through "layering," or rooting of lower branches.

Like most of the timberline conifers, alpine larch has thin bark and is rather easily killed by fire; however fire has little overall effect on this species because of the broken, rocky terrain, sparse fuels, and short burning season where it grows. Man's activities also have had very little effect on this high mountain tree, although alpine larch may have had more effect upon men. Those who have come to know it will long remember how its golden color highlights the high country at the close of summer, how old lumpy larch limbs crackle in a mountain campfire, and how a soft breeze stirs the wispy boughs overhead, setting them in motion across a background of starlight.

Sitka Spruce

Picea sitchensis
Pine family *(Pinaceae)*

Sitka spruce is a large forest tree that grows along nearly 2000 miles of the North Pacific shore but seldom occurs more than a few dozen miles inland from salt water. It extends northward along the coast from northern California through Oregon, Washington, British Columbia, and Alaska to Kodiak Island, reaching farther north and west along the coast (into the tundra) than any other conifer. Named for Sitka, Alaska, it is the most important commercial timber species in the 49th State.

Its other common name "tideland spruce" aptly describes its habitat in the cold, wet North Pacific fog belt, where annual rainfall is generally 60 to 200 inches, making it the wettest area in North America. Temperatures in the Sitka spruce forest zone, even in Alaska, seldom fall below zero degrees F., and the ocean's moderating influence keeps the warmest summer month at a relatively cool average temperature of about 60° F. (16 C.).

Unlike other conifers, that grow at progressively higher elevations southward, Sitka spruce becomes restricted to a narrower band along the coastal lowlands going south. It covers the entire forest zone from sea level to timberline (averaging about 3000 feet) on the Alaskan Coast, but is restricted in our area to the lowlands, seldom extending above 1500 feet in elevation. In northern California Sitka spruce is confined to narrow strips along coastal streams within a few hundred feet of sea level.

Sitka spruce is abundant near the ocean, often growing as stout, limby trees atop the wind-battered cliffs or clinging to the crest of rock islands known as "sea stacks." Some of these ocean-side trees develop huge burls on their trunks, the cause of which remains unknown. One spruce on the Washington coast was 3

Sitka spruce burls and growth forms in oceanside conditions

feet thick but supported a burl nearly 7 feet across.

From Alaska to Oregon, countless thousands of bald eagles roost in these coastline spruces, surveying the breakers for morsels of seafood. Sitka spruce also extends up the major river valleys into the coastal mountains and the Washington Cascades. It penetrates 100 miles up the Frazer and Columbia Rivers, and occurs on the Snoqualmie River, along Interstate 90, within a few miles of Snoqualmie Pass. South of the Columbia it is restricted to within a few miles of the coast; yet the largest-known Sitka spruce grows in coastal Oregon.

Sitka spruce often becomes a massive tree limbed nearly to the ground with branches 8 inches thick and 30 feet long. These great, spreading boughs often have secondary branches that hang down 2 or 3 feet in a weeping appearance. Open-grown spruce with their huge, limby crowns, called "wolf trees," make good shelter from the rain (provided one has enough time for waiting out the rain; a bedroll, food, and several good books may come in handy).

Sitka spruce ranks with Douglas-fir and western redcedar as the Northwest's largest trees. In fact, these three species are

among the world's largest, after California's redwood and sequoia. Spruce 8 feet thick and over 200 feet tall are commonly
encountered in the old-growth stands of the coastal Northwest.
Oregon and Washington have a long-standing "biggest-tree"
contest: Oregon currently claims the record Sitka spruce —
16½ feet thick and 216 feet tall where broken off, with a maximum crown spread of 93 feet. This gigantic specimen stands in a
small park on Highway 26 south of Seaside. The Washington runner-up, only slightly smaller, grows along the Hoh River
near Highway 101.

The tops of most of the large coastal trees have been sheared
off in winter hurricanes, but in the more sheltered valleys, such
as up the Hoh River in Olympic National Park, the very tallest
spruce reach 300 feet into the soggy atmosphere. The ability of
trees to pump sap and nutrients (or, rather, to pull it up through
microscopically-thin capillary tubes) to such heights has long
amazed physicists; only five species of trees in the world (including Douglas-fir, redwood, sequoia, and an Australian eucalyptus)
are known to achieve this height.

One might expect such large trees to be 1000 years or older, but
Sitka spruce attains these gargantuan dimensions in much less
time. On good sites such as valley bottoms, it may reach 175 feet
or more in 100 years. This vigorous growth also characterizes
Sitka spruce in the damp English countryside; thus it has become a favorite for forest plantations in the British Isles. The
largest spruce in our Northwest forests are generally 400 to 700
years old, and some of them are still growing rapidly. A tree near
the Queets River Campground in Olympic National Park is 13½
feet thick, with almost no basal swelling, but it is estimated to be
only about 400 years of age. An increment core — a pencil-
shaped piece of wood taken with a hollow drill — extracted on a
research study revealed that this Sitka spruce is adding a foot to
its massive diameter every 30 to 35 years!

The coastal valleys dominated by large Sitka spruce have been
called temperate-zone rain forests. In addition to the towering
conifers, these habitats are characterized by a thick, spongy car-
pet of moss covering the entire forest floor. Moss even hangs in
heavy drapes from the limbs of the bigleaf maples. Conifer seedlings cannot ordinarily grow in this moss; but they can get established on rotten logs, atop stumps, and even in the clods of dirt

clinging to roots of overthrown trees. Only in such an ultra-humid environment is it possible — or necessary — for conifers to get established on these unusual "microsites." That most Sitka spruce in the rain forest got their start on such microsites is evident by the way their trunks are raised off the ground on stilted root systems. These roots once spanned a log or stump, which rotted away in a century or two. Sometimes the roots hold the trunk 6 or 8 feet up in the air, and often several large trees are obviously lined up in a row or "colonnade" because they started as seedlings on the same rotten log.

These temperate rain forests occur in sheltered coastal valleys from the Alaska Panhandle to northern Oregon, where annual precipitation is well over 100 inches. Sitka spruce's major associate is western hemlock, a tree that is very tolerant of shade. Without disturbances such as blowdowns, fire, or logging, spruce replaces itself through seedlings less effectively than western hemlock, but its lifespan is great enough to almost insure that disturbances will eventually leave openings for its regeneration. When such an opening appears, young spruce will usually fill it, far outstripping hemlock in height growth.

Sitka spruce have shallow root systems, and violent coastal storms often wrench huge trees out of the ground, or snap their trunks off. Sitka spruce's bark is thin and provides little protection against the intense forest fires that develop on the rare occasions when the luxuriant vegetation dries out and a lightning storm or other ignition source happens along. Less than five electrical storms per year are recorded at sites in the Sitka spruce forest zone; mankind now inadvertently sets most of the fires.

Sitka spruce bark is distinct from that of other coastal conifers in being purplish or reddish brown and broken into large loose scales. The foliage contrasts with that of other coastal trees since the needles are stiff and prickly to the touch. Sitka spruce needles are flattened, and will not readily roll between one's fingers, unlike those of the other spruces — which grow inland from the Pacific. The cones are 2½ to 4 inches long and are composed of tan, papery scales. The seeds are tiny (210,000 per pound) and can be carried considerable distances by the wind.

Columbian black-tailed deer and Roosevelt elk that live in Sitka spruce country seem to relish the succulent new shoots on sap-

Sitka spruce

lings in early spring, but the needles soon harden off to prickly sharpness. Coastal Indians wove baskets and rain hats out of the fine pliable roots of Sitka spruce. They used spruce pitch for calking canoes, and had a variety of medicinal uses for parts of this tree. Some pioneers in the Hoh River Valley of western Washington split shakes for siding and roofing from Sitka spruce.

Both Indians and modern campers have found that big Sitka spruce limbs are dense and resinous, and produce a hot, long-lasting campfire. By contrast, the trunk wood is light, and burns more quickly. But it has other uses: although light in weight, Sitka spruce wood is stiff, comparatively strong, and resilient, and thus is well suited for shelving, ladders, folding bleachers, and racing shells. However, it is most famous for its use as the prime source of wood for airplanes. This species is said to have supplied most of the wood used by the American, British, and French air forces in World Wars I and II. (One reporter suggested that it proved hazardous to aviators when it was being splintered by enemy bullets, not mentioning dangers presented by the bullets themselves!) The Sitka spruce forests were heavily logged during the war years in order to obtain the very small percentage of flawless wood that could qualify for airplanes. Fortunately it is not in such great demand for modern aircraft.

Sitka spruce wood also has high resonant qualities and thus is used in musical instruments. Several years ago a single "select" grade Sitka spruce log, suitable for these instruments, was reportedly purchased by the Japanese from a Hoh River landowner for $1,400. Resonant Sitka spruce wood is also used for the sounding boards that guide ships through fog-bound waterways such as the inlets along which this tree grows on the damp coast of the North Pacific.

Engelmann Spruce

Picea engelmannii
Pine family *(Pinaceae)*

Engelmann spruce typically dominates wet sites in the high mountains east of the Cascade Crest. Old-growth spruce usually tower above all other species growing along streams and in moist basins in the subalpine forest, and extend down to lower elevations in frost pockets and moist canyons, reaching as low as 1700 feet in extreme northern Idaho and interior British Columbia. At the opposite extreme, Engelmann spruce forms part of the alpine timberline as high as 9000 feet elevation in the inland Northwest, and attains 12,000 feet at its upper limits in Colorado, where it is the principal tree at high altitudes.

"Spruce bottoms" dominated by this species extend up along the mountain streams in all of the 11 western states except California and Nevada, where it is rare. Engelmann spruce also spreads northward in the inland mountains to central British Columbia. In Northwest forests it is most abundant between about 3000 and 7000 feet elevation on moist sites. Nevertheless, it is scattered in small quantities over a much broader range of conditions, including dry sites at high elevations.

Although Engelmann spruce can readily be seen throughout the moister mountain forests of the interior Northwest, it is most accessible to residents of the Pacific Slope via passes in the Cascades. Such locations include Manning Provincial Park in British Columbia, Early Winters Creek on the North Cascades Highway in Washington, White River and Yakima Park on Mount Rainier, and the Loop Road around Mount Hood.

Engelmann spruce, in sharp contrast to Sitka spruce, is intolerant of the oceanic climate and seldom grows very far west of the Cascade Divide. It was thought to be entirely absent from the

coast ranges of Oregon and Washington, but within the last decade a few small stands have been discovered high up in the
canyons of the northeastern Olympic Mountains, in the relatively dry "rain-shadow zone." These groves are not of recent
origin as is evidenced by the fact that one of them, on Cameron
Creek, contains an Engelmann spruce 7 feet thick and 179 feet
tall — nearly as large as the largest-known Engelmann spruce,
found in Idaho.

Typical old-growth Engelmann spruce in high basins are 3
feet thick and 120 to 140 feet tall. Even near timberline, on
sheltered sites, these spruce often stand 80 to 90 feet high —
considerably taller than their associates, subalpine fir and whitebark pine. However, unlike Sitka spruce, it takes a long time
(often 300 years) for Engelmann spruce to achieve such a dominant stature. Judging from analysis of annual rings, these trees
grow slowly, but remarkably steadily, for up to 400 or 500 years
before a windstorm, spruce beetle outbreak, or fire starts the
recycling process.

Engelmann spruce is readily recognized at a distance by its
tall, narrow crown (not as sharp-pointed as that of subalpine fir)
with thousands of tassel-like branchlets hanging down from the
main limbs. Open-grown trees are heavily limbed to the ground.
The distinctive bark is very thin, with a dark purplish or reddish
tinge. Also it has loose scales that flake off readily, a trait evident
even on trees only 3 inches thick.

Like all other North American spruces, it has stout, prickly
needles; this is why gardeners often choose spruce for an impenetrable evergreen hedge. Engelmann spruce needles are
four-sided and can be rolled between one's fingers. Like those of
other spruces, the needles are attached to the twigs by small
wooden pegs which remain after the needles fall, giving old
twigs a warty texture. The needles give off a strong resinous
odor when crushed, and the foliage of vigorous young trees is
often noticeably bluish — resembling the Colorado blue spruce
(Picea pungens) which is so commonly used for landscaping.

Engelmann spruce often has two different types of cone-like
structures hanging from its boughs, but one of these is really an
aphid gall. What appear at first to be pointed scales are dried-up
needles protruding from the multi-chambered house of the
Cooley gall aphid. While the galls are still soft, several tiny white
aphids live in each chamber; after the insects have left, the galls

Engelmann spruce

dry out, harden, and turn brown. They remain on the branches for many years.

In late spring plump, purple pollen cones about ½ inch long appear on branch-tips all over the trees. Watch an open-growing spruce in a spring breeze and you'll see a yellow cloud of pollen burst into the air with every gust of wind. Heavy crops of female or seed-bearing cones can often be seen in the upper crown. They are bright red at first, turning purple for most of the summer, and drying to a tan color in the fall. They are generally shorter than cones of Sitka spruce, ranging from 1 to 2½ inches in length.

At low elevations in the interior of British Columbia and in northwestern Montana, Engelmann spruce hybridizes extensively with white spruce *(Picea glauca),* a tree of northern and eastern Canada and the northeastern United States. The hybrids have cone characteristics and other features intermediate between those of pure Engelmann spruce and pure white spruce. Typical Engelmann spruce cones have wrinkled, rather pointed scales with an uneven margin; by contrast white spruce cones have flat, broad, rounded scales with a smooth margin. Engelmann spruce cones are harvested in quantity by red squirrels, but the seeds are so small that many of them are scattered about and overlooked in the process. Evidently they may sometimes lie dormant in the forest-floor duff for a few years before germinating. The seedling can survive and grow up slowly beneath a dense, shady canopy, then respond with faster growth if the overstory thins out.

Because of their great height, relatively dense crown, and shallow root systems, large Engelmann spruce in the high mountains are often broken off or uprooted by violent windstorms. Their lofty crowns also invite lightning strikes, as witnessed by the scar spiraling down the trunk of many a veteran spruce in the high country. Sometimes a big old spruce is literally blasted apart by lightning, with massive splinters sent crashing off in all directions (it behooves a hiker to keep away from tall trees during an electrical storm).

Wind-shaped Engelmann spruce at timberline

As one might suspect, this densely limbed, thin-barked tree is readily killed by forest fire; but the "bottoms" where it is most abundant often escape burning because of their moist conditions. At least two much-sought-after types of wild creatures are especially prevalent in spruce bottoms. Plump native trout lurk in the quiet pools in the streams among the undercut spruce roots, and in southern British Columbia, Idaho, Montana, and Wyoming, moose often spend much of the year foraging and bedding down beneath the somber canopy formed by towering

Engelmann spruce.

The wood of this species is creamy white in color, very light in weight (21½ pounds per cubic foot), stiff, and moderately strong. It is used for poles, boards, and many of the purposes described for Sitka spruce. Since it has no odor and very little pitch, it has been used for food containers, including barrels. Like spruces of the Northeast and Canada, one of its principal products is the pulp that it yields for paper, from newsprint to high-grade writing stock.

Douglas-fir

Pseudotsuga menziesii
Pine family *(Pinaceae)*

Douglas-fir yields more timber than any other species in North America, and although it grows throughout much of the western half of the continent, it reaches great size only in the coastal Northwest, and is probably more familiar to Northwesterners than any other tree. It serves as the usual Christmas tree in our region and is also shipped by the hundreds of thousands across the country in refrigerated cars. Douglas-fir is the vigorous, dense-crowned evergreen that soon covers cut-over lands west of the Cascade Divide, and it is the large tree with heavily furrowed bark found in our city parks and lowland forests.

Thus it seems ironic that this outstanding and very distinctive tree has an obscure identity, but the confusion is rooted deep in history. These huge, corky-barked trees were discovered in 1791 on the coast of Vancouver Island by the Scottish physician and naturalist Dr. Archibald Menzies, who was accompanying Captain George Vancouver on his explorations. Three decades later another Scotsman, David Douglas, found this tree in Oregon.

At first botanists classified it as a pine, and it gained the common name "Oregon pine." However, this magnificent conifer does not bear needles in clusters like pines, nor does it have pine-like cones. Bark on the young trees is smooth and pocked with balsam blisters like that of the firs *(Abies)*; the pointed, inch-long needles somewhat resemble spruce *(Picea)* or yew *(Taxus)*, and the cones look like chubby spruce cones except for unique three-pronged, fork-like bracts that project from between the scales. Naturalist John Muir called it "Douglas Spruce," and it was classified as a true fir and as a hemlock *(Tsuga)* in botanical literature in the 1800s.

Then botanists exploring the Himalayas and mountains of China and Japan brought back samples of other trees like "Oregon pine," and in 1867 the technical name *Pseudotsuga*, meaning "false hemlock," was proposed for this singular group of trees. At first our "Oregon pine" was classified *Pseudotsuga douglasii* in honor of David Douglas. Later this was replaced by *Pseudotsuga taxifolia* ("false hemlock with leaves like a yew") since this name was based upon a prior reference in botanical literature. However, in 1950 another botanist discovered that the original reference supporting that name had not been recorded properly under the international rules of plant nomenclature. Consequently, he renamed the tree *Pseudotsuga menziesii* based upon the next oldest name.

Thus the botanical name now acknowledges the original discoverer, while the accepted common name, "Douglas-fir," is applied to all of the several members of the genus *Pseudotsuga*. Hopefully, at last the nomenclature of this species is resolved, and that is why Douglas-fir (or "Douglasfir") cannot correctly be written as two words — the tree simply is not any kind of a "fir" *(Abies)*. The only other *Pseudotsuga* in the Western Hemisphere is a smaller tree bearing larger cones that grows in the mountains of southern California; it is called "bigcone Douglas-fir" *(Pseudotsuga macrocarpa)*.

Douglas-fir grows from central British Columbia southward in the coastal states to central California, extends southward in the Rockies through Arizona and New Mexico, and into the high mountains of subtropical Mexico. From Puget Sound area northward it occurs mostly between sea level and 4000 feet elevation. Farther south, as well as east of the Cascades, it often ascends to 5000 or 6000 feet. In the Colorado Rockies Douglas-fir typically grows between elevations of 8000 and 10,000 feet.

As one might suspect, coastal Douglas-fir is significantly different from the inland or Rocky Mountain form. The former is adapted to a moist, mild climate where it grows rapidly, attaining heights of 200 feet or more and diameters of 4 to 8 feet on favorable sites. By contrast Rocky Mountain Douglas-fir endures much colder and drier conditions, and grows slowly, seldom exceeding 130 feet in height. Except for their size, the two forms do not differ greatly in appearance, although the inland form tends to have bluish-green foliage (vs. yellowish-green for coas-

tal Douglas-fir) and smaller cones on which the three-pronged bracts are often bent backwards.

In addition to its unique cones with the forked bracts, Douglas-fir has several other characteristics that make identification easy. All Douglas-firs from small trees to rotten stumps have a corky textured bark (or remnants of it) which, when cut with a knife, shows wavy bands of tan and dark brown, somewhat like the pattern in a pile of bacon slices. Buds at the tip of Douglas-fir

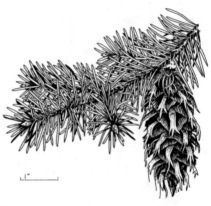

Douglas-fir

branches are another key feature: they are sharp pointed and covered with dark-brown overlapping scales. In contrast, buds of the true firs (*Abies*) are light colored, blunt, and waxy. As Christmas tree and bough gatherers readily notice, Douglas-fir foliage has a delightful and distinctive resinous fragrance. Using these characteristics, there is no need to confuse Douglas-fir with any other species. Ironically, however, many a forestry student misidentifies this commonest of Northwest trees because he looked only at the somewhat variable needles.

When foresters reminisce about coastal Douglas-fir there are bound to be stories about its phenomenal growth-rate or the thousand-year-old giant whose butt log was almost too big to fit by itself on a large logging truck. Many years ago a forestry class inspecting a stand of second-growth Douglas-fir on a good site west of Olympia, Washington, was amazed to find that a tree 3 feet thick and 170 feet tall was a mere 72 years of age. In the early 1960s a Douglas-fir from southwestern British Columbia was cut into a 225-foot-long flagpole and shipped to England, after an unusual trip out of the woods lashed to the top of two oversized logging trucks. An even longer Douglas-fir flagpole (299½ feet) was proudly displayed at the Oregon building in the Panama-Pacific International exposition of 1915. Douglas-firs 300 feet in height have been discovered at several locations in southwestern British Columbia, western Washington, and western Oregon, but perhaps the most intriguing big-tree epic is the fateful tale of the world record Douglas-fir.

In the early 1950s a massive Douglas-fir was discovered growing in the remote Queets River Valley in Olympic National Park. This tree was 14½ feet thick with a clear, pillar-like trunk having but little taper. The top was broken off at 221 feet. The American Forestry Association declared this "Queets Fir" as the national champion.

Oregonians took note and kept watch for a bigger Douglas-fir in their State. About 10 years later they found the "Clatsop Fir," and an official surveying party soon determined that it had an even greater girth, although its volume was less than the 14,000 cubic feet of the Queets Fir. A good-natured controversy arose about which State was entitled to claim the largest of all Douglas-firs. Nature settled that matter shortly.

Columbus Day 1962 brought hurricane winds that blew down 10 billion board feet of timber in Oregon and Washington; but both champion Douglas-firs stood fast. Then a lesser storm the same winter toppled the Clatsop Fir.

Thus the Queets Fir reigned unchallenged until 1975. That spring a forester named Finnegan working out of Coos Bay, Oregon, found a Douglas-fir over 13 feet thick and with an undamaged top 302 feet tall. Based on its formula considering diameter, height, and crown spread, the American Forestry Association declared Finnegan's Fir to be the new national champion. Ironically, although this tree had stood for an estimated 800 to 1000 years, it blew over in a hurricane that November. Its remains proved to be a thin skin of sound wood surrounding a huge mass of rot. So, again, the Queets Fir reigns, and Oregonians are out combing their wet coastal valleys looking for a bigger one!

The corky bark of veteran coastal Douglas-firs may be as much

Witches brooms in Douglas-fir; close-up
of dwarfmistletoe in Douglas-fir twig

as a foot thick. This insulation coupled with the long, clear trunk provides considerable protection against fire. Historically, forest fires and perhaps massive blowdowns have helped perpetuate stands of Douglas-fir. These trees are less tolerant of shade than the western hemlock and western redcedar with which they usually grow. Consequently, without some form of disturbance every few hundred years, hemlock continues regenerating and gradually becomes dominant in the stand. The Queets Fir is one of few 1000-year-old survivors of a Douglas-fir stand that has since given way to hemlocks.

When a fire, clearcut, or other disturbance occurs, Douglas-fir usually seeds in from surviving veterans or from the surrounding stand, and outstrips its competitors to gain dominance in the new stand. Experiments have shown that sizeable quantities of winged Douglas-fir seed (42,000 per pound) are spread ¼ mile downwind from the parent tree in just a moderate breeze.

Douglas-fir's abundance throughout the coastal and mountainous West can be explained by its adaptability. Douglas-fir is probably a member of more different forest types than any other species. It prospers under a wide range of climatic conditions. It can survive both drought and fire, and regenerates vigorously following disturbances. It is long-lived, tough, and durable. Also, in the inland forests it is more tolerant of shade than many of its associates (e.g., ponderosa pine, western larch, and lodgepole pine).

Douglas-fir is one of the easier species to transplant and to cultivate under a variety of conditions. Seed brought back to England by David Douglas in 1827 produced trees that became the forerunners of extensive plantations there.

While Douglas-fir is perhaps the best-adapted all-around tree in the West, there is even less room for question regarding the value of its wood. By the turn of the century it had replaced white pine as the prime industrial timber, since it grows in vast forests of larger trees. The wood is of medium weight, and is moderately hard and strong. It makes an excellent structural material also because it is available in high-grade stock in large sizes. It is a prime material for plywood as well as for a variety of other forest products. Additionally, it makes good firewood, and slabs of the thick bark make excellent coals.

Humans are not the only creatures in the Northwest that depend upon Douglas-fir. Douglas squirrels harvest great quantities of cones. Chipmunks, meadow mice, deer mice, and shrews

Squirrel's forgotten cache

eat seed that has fallen from the trees. The seed also forms an important part of the diet for crossbills, winter wrens, and song sparrows. Deer eat the new shoots of Douglas-fir, and black bears often strip the bark of vigorous young trees to eat the sap layer or cambium. Added to this list are significant depredations by various insects such as the western budworm, tussock moth, and Douglas-fir beetle, parasites like the dwarfmistletoe *(Arceuthobium douglasii)* plant, and several root and stem-rotting fungi. Thus dependence on Douglas-fir is indeed heavy. Fortunately this species is a very capable provider.

Western Hemlock

Tsuga heterophylla
Pine family *(Pinaceae)*

Western hemlock is seemingly an example of the "meek that inherit the earth." This species seems inconspicuous among the gigantic Douglas-fir, Sitka spruce, and western redcedar of the coastal Northwest forests. But, despite the fact that it grows more slowly and attains smaller size and lesser age than its associates, it can eventually dominate most of the coastal forest belt.

Besides its prolific seed crops, western hemlock's key advantage over the other species is the ability of its seedlings to grow up under dense shade. Its principal associates need a fire, blowdown, logging, or other disturbance to create some open ground, preferably with bare, mineral soil, for their seedlings. By contrast, perhaps the most impressive display of western hemlock regeneration is the hundreds of seedlings that can be found carpeting a rotting log lying beneath the somber canopy of a stand in the coastal rain forest. Nearly all of such seedlings are likely to be western hemlock even if Douglas-fir or Sitka spruce dominate the tall-tree layer of the overstory.

If several centuries pass without a major disturbance, western hemlock gradually replaces the other conifers in the stand. After perhaps 1000 years the spruce and even the veteran Douglas-firs will have toppled in old age, and a "climax" or self-perpetuating forest type of essentially pure western hemlock is the result. Of course such immense periods without fire, hurricane blowdowns, floods, or logging are rare on most of the coastal forest landscape, and so most stands have a mixture of tree species. Still, whenever one walks through an old-growth stand, chances are that he will find western hemlock saplings far outnumber those of other species.

While the coastal Northwest is the heart of western hemlock country, this species extends northward at lower elevations along the Pacific to south-central Alaska, and southward into the fog-bound redwood coast of northern California. It grows on all but the soggiest sites and the driest areas west of the Cascade Divide from southern British Columbia to west-central Oregon, being abundant up to about 3500 feet in elevation. It also occurs inland in the wettest area of the Rocky Mountain System in southeastern British Columbia, northeastern Washington, northern Idaho, and northwestern Montana. In that area it forms the potential climax in the productive western white pine timber type, which is restricted to moist valleys and north-facing slopes at lower elevations (under 5000 feet).

Most western hemlock forests harbor luxuriant undergrowth consisting of such species as vine maple, rhododendron, salal, evergreen huckleberry, and sword fern. Shrubs become especially dense on cut-over sites, along with a jungle-like growth of red alder, salmonberry, and bracken fern. But, by the time western hemlock has formed a dense canopy, so little light penetrates it that only sparse undergrowth (including seedlings and saplings of hemlock) survives. Pure stands of this species are so densely stocked that despite the tree's modest proportions, an acre of 100-year-old western hemlock forest can yield even more timber (150,000 to 190,000 board feet on a good site) than a comparable stand of the larger, but less densely crowded Douglas-fir.

Many Northwesterners recognize smaller western hemlock trees by the way their growing tips droop. This tree's foliage itself is also distinctive. The needles are small, flat, blunt, and of unequal lengths, but always rather short. The species name *heterophylla* means "variable leaves"; ranging from ¼ to ¾ of an inch in length, they have white bands on the underside, and grow in a somewhat two-ranked pattern, from opposite sides of the branch. The fine foliage and branching arrangement gives the boughs a delicate spray-like appearance unlike other needle-leaved conifers.

The cones, also small and delicate, are often borne in large quantities on the branchlets. They are tan and papery and less than 1 inch long when mature, and they are produced in such profusion that they cover the forest floor. A western hemlock

Western hemlock

cone holds 30 to 40 tiny seeds (300,000 per pound), each having a membraneous wing. Experiments have shown that some western hemlock seed travels half a mile from the parent tree in only a light wind. This species begins yielding cone crops at age 25 or 30, and, thereafter outproduces all of its associates. In an Oregon stand foresters discovered that an average of eight million western hemlock seeds per acre were produced annually.

Despite their small size, these seeds can germinate and grow into successful trees on substrates ranging from mineral soil to moss, decaying litter, or rotten stumps. The seedling's main requirement is that the rooting medium stay moist, because the plant is not drought-resistant and its roots develop slowly. A small western hemlock tree is sometimes found perched atop a rotten stump 15 or 20 feet above the forest floor; inspection will reveal that one or more roots extend down the stump into the damp soil.

Hemlock seedlings are capable of surviving at a very slow rate of growth for decades. A favorable event such as the toppling of a large tree gives some of them the opportunity to grow more rapidly and reach into the forest canopy. However, on cleared or burned sites western hemlock seedlings do not compete in initial height growth with red alder, Douglas-fir, Sitka spruce, and other species, and they may be damaged by excessive exposure to the drying sun. But after the other species have become well established, the shade they cast is favorable to western hemlock, which then increases in the understory.

Favorable sites in southwestern British Columbia, western Washington, and western Oregon produce old-growth western hemlock 3 to 4 feet thick and up to 200 feet tall. This species is reported to attain a maximum age of about 500 years, relatively modest by standards of the West Coast forest. Old trees are often heavily infected with various trunk, butt, or root-rotting fungi, or with dwarf-mistletoe. Outbreaks of black-headed budworm and hemlock looper are often destructive to hemlock forests, and very old trees are ultimately snapped off or uprooted by strong winds, especially when coupled with heavy loads of clinging wet snow. These trees are particularly susceptible to being overthrown because of their shallow rooting habit, and with their thin bark and dense foliage, have little chance of surviving a forest fire.

Until about 1920 this species was regarded as a "weed tree" from the commercial timber standpoint, apparently because lumbermen assumed that its wood was similar to that of the eastern hemlock (*Tsuga canadensis*). Later they learned that western hemlock wood is substantially better than its eastern kin from almost all standpoints. In fact, this wood is well suited for a wide range of uses, including flooring for gymnasiums. Western hemlock also makes excellent wood pulp for paper production, and serves as the principal source of alpha cellulose fiber used in the manufacture of rayon, cellophane, and many plastics. The bark is rich in tannin, used in making leather.

Thus, although western hemlock is not as spectacular as some of its principal associates, it has proven to be a "Cinderella tree" from the commercial viewpoint, and its biological importance in Northwest forests is also well established.

Mountain Hemlock

Tsuga mertensiana
Pine family (*Pinaceae*)

Mountain hemlock is a handsome tree with luxuriant foliage and dark, furrowed bark that characterizes the deep-snow high country of the Pacific Coast mountains. Throughout its natural distribution mountain hemlock grows almost exclusively in the uppermost forest zone. At its northern limits on the snowy Alaska coast near Seward, it grows predominantly with Sitka spruce and extends from just above sea level to the limit of trees, which is just under 2000 feet elevation. Southward in the Alaska Panhandle and coastal British Columbia, the mountain hemlock zone rises in elevation, occurring above the Sitka spruce-western hemlock forest.

From southwestern British Columbia to northwestern Oregon, mountain hemlock forest extends from about 3500 feet elevation to the limit of trees, near 6000 feet. It occurs at still higher altitudes in southern Oregon, where beautiful stands dominate the rim above Crater Lake. Mountain hemlock forest borders the ski slopes on Mount Shasta in northern California, and this species also occupies the snowiest parts of the northern Sierra Nevada mountains; but southward in that range it becomes restricted to moist, sheltered cirque basins and stream borders near the 10,000-foot level. Mountain hemlock reaches its southern limits there, at about the same latitude as the southernmost glaciers in North America. This tree also extends eastward from our Northwest coastal mountains into the wettest inland ranges, but it is widespread and abundant only in the snowy Selkirks of southeastern British Columbia and the northern part of Idaho's Bitterroot Mountains.

Mountain hemlock occupies the snowiest forests in North

America. Average annual snowfall ranges from about 32 to 50 feet at the principal weather stations, and the station at Paradise on Mount Rainier has been deluged with world-record snowfalls of 90 feet in a single winter season. Moreover, this is not light powder; it is heavy, wet snow, yielding massive quantities of runoff when it melts in late spring and early summer, often washed into the soil and down the waterways with copious rains. Thus, it is easy to see why mountain hemlock is described as a tree of the wet, snowy mountains.

Considering its snowy habitat, one might expect mountain hemlock to have a compact, narrow crown like subalpine fir or Engelmann spruce, so that snow loads would not accumulate so heavily and damage the tree. Young hemlocks do indeed have a narrowly pyramidal crown; but as they mature these trees often develop large crowns composed of great, spreading branches, upon which huge quantities of snow collect. Therefore, it behooves a spring skier to avoid resting under the "umbrella" of a big old hemlock on a warm afternoon!

Groves of slender, pole-size mountain hemlocks grow on sites where they are flattened each winter by the snow pack sliding down from steep slopes above. On July afternoons, hikers often witness these young trees literally popping up out of their winter

Young, limber mountain hemlock under heavy snowpack

tombs of melting snowpack. Trees on steep slopes typically have a base that arches downslope before bending back up vertically; this condition, known as "pistol butt," is caused by creeping snow.

Mountain hemlock foliage is quite different from that of western hemlock and of the two other American hemlocks, which grow in the East. Its needles are plump, and they spread out in clusters

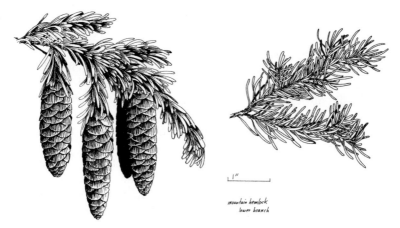

Mountain hemlock: cone-bearing foliage and twig from lower branch

from all sides of little spur shoots, giving the twigs a luxuriant, bushy appearance. In contrast, western hemlock has flat needles that are arranged in flat, open sprays. Mountain hemlock foliage is often bluish-green, while western hemlock is yellowish green. Mountain hemlock cones are generally 1½ to 2 inches long, while those of other hemlocks are an inch or less. Also mountain hemlock's bark is thicker and more heavily furrowed than that of its relatives. Occasionally trees having characteristics intermediate between mountain and western hemlock are found where the two species' elevational ranges overlap (usually 3000 to 3500 feet). Studies have found that most of these "intermediate" trees are probably western hemlocks which may have adapted to the snow-forest environment by acquiring some growth characteristics similar to those of mountain hemlock.

The shape and arrangement of the needles and the comparatively large cones of mountain hemlock are characteristics resembling spruce (*Picea*) more than other hemlocks; thus it is not surprising that early naturalists often regarded it as a spruce. For instance, John Muir referred to this species as the "Hemlock Spruce." In 1949 a French botanist theorized that mountain hemlock was actually a hybrid of spruce and hemlock, but more recently, detailed genetic studies have tended to confirm that it is indeed a true hemlock. A point of confusion about "hemlock" itself is its false identification with the fatal potion that Socrates drank; "poison hemlock" is actually an herb in the parsley family.

Mountain hemlock takes on a variety of growth forms to adapt to high-country conditions. Below about 4000 feet elevation in our coastal mountains, it grows in dense stands with subalpine fir, Pacific silver fir, and Alaska-cedar, reaching diameters of 3 to 4 feet and, under the best conditions, heights up to 150 feet. Mountain hemlock and all of these associates are very tolerant of shade, so the forest canopy is often dense indeed.

Higher up, where excessive snow and wind tends to break up the forest, mountain hemlock forms a mosaic with patches of mountain heath (*Phyllodoce* and *Cassiope*), meadows, rockpiles, and small lakes. In this timberline belt, mountain hemlock often grows as stout, isolated trees with large wind-battered crowns and thick, gnarled trunks. Smaller hemlocks often surround these 500-year-old veterans; the former are slender and graceful by comparison. The lush mountain hemlock boughs are often covered with generous quantities of the purple to brownish cones. At the limit of trees, mountain hemlock may grow as a huge, sprawling shrub with so many upturned branch-trunks that one tree simulates a small grove.

Thus this species has picturesque growth forms ranging from wind-sheared alpine scrub and natural "bonsai" miniatures to graceful or giant trees. At timberline they are found in a flower-filled setting with glistening water, rock, and snowfields. Such habitats may resemble a collection of Japanese gardens, and this likeness is not accidental. Hemlocks from Oriental mountain forests have long been a favorite of Japanese horticulturists. Moreover, mountain hemlock has been used for landscaping in the Northwest and throughout Great Britain, where it was first cultivated via seed brought back from the Mount Baker area in the 1850s.

Mountain hemlock does not survive in the drier inland mountains, presumably because of low winter temperatures coupled with drying winds and a lack of protective snowcover. But in the coastal mountains it can grow on the rockiest soils, including even recent lava flows, if moisture is adequate. For instance, the southernmost grove—at 10,000 feet in Sequoia National Park, California—is situated essentially on bedrock, but has springs flowing all through it in mid-summer.

Wind-sheared alpine scrub

Not surprisingly, mountain hemlock seedlings are often the first trees to invade heathland and glacial moraines at timberline. Although its seed crops tend to be ample, this species also regenerates extensively through "layering." That is, lower branches of older trees, that are in contact with the ground, take root and then grow erect to become trees. This is an effective means of regenerating at timberline since layered saplings are sheltered by the growth of the parent tree, and initially receive their nutrients through the established root system of the old tree.

In the forest proper, mountain hemlock's canopy is so dense that it is said to have inspired the logger's common name "black hemlock" for this species. The tree is harvested only to a limited extent, near its lower limits, and the wood is generally mixed with western hemlock in marketing. Fire and blowdowns are usually not extensive in these high-elevation coastal forests, thus the stands can often progress toward a "climax" or stabilized condition. Mountain hemlock is about as tolerant of dense shade as its principal associates with the exception of Pacific silver fir. Therefore, it is a dominant in climax forests, except near its lower limits where Pacific silver fir can eventually largely replace it. But then, as usual, a share of factors work to counterbalance dominance by Pacific silver fir, which is the next tree in our discussion.

Pacific Silver Fir

Abies amabilis
Pine family (*Pinaceae*)

Pacific silver fir is a handsome tree that inhabits the middle and upper elevations in the moist mountain ranges bordering the North Pacific Ocean. This tree's distribution extends from the southern tip of the Alaska Panhandle along the coast ranges and the Cascades almost to Crater Lake, Oregon. A few isolated groves have also been found in the Klamath Mountains of northwestern California. Pacific silver fir reaches its best development, and is a dominant species in the west-slope forests from southwestern British Columbia to northern Oregon, mostly between 2000 and 5000 feet elevation. It generally grows in areas receiving more than 60 inches of annual precipitation, and does not inhabit even the wettest mountain ranges east of the Cascades.

This tree's scientific name means "lovely fir," and its foliage is indeed strikingly beautiful. The branches are clothed with blunt, inch-long needles that are lustrous dark green above and silvery white beneath. The leaves extend from opposite sides of the branch, and are also brushed forward along the top of the twig, giving the foliage a ruffled appearance. The result is a luxuriant, flattened spray that is shiny green above and silvery on its underside.

Like all true or balsam firs (genus *Abies*), Pacific silver fir produces a second type of foliage in its top, on the cone-bearing branches. These needles are stout, curved, and very sharp; thus they often confuse the beginning botanist who finds a broken tree-top lying on the forest floor. However, the tree-top does provide one excellent clue to the identity of this and other true firs. In summer during the infrequent cone-crop years, it has

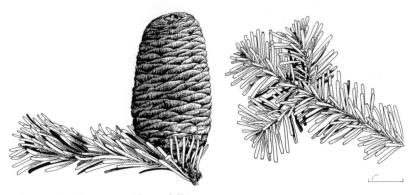

Pacific silver fir: cone and lower foliage

distinctive barrel-shaped cones sitting stiffly erect in the upper-most boughs. (Northwesterners may note the resemblance of these erect fir cones to those found in abundance on the deodar and Atlas cedars (genus *Cedrus*), native to the Himalayas and the Mediterranean region, which are commonly cultivated in cities west of the Cascades.) Cones of all the true firs dry out and fall apart at maturity in early autumn; however the spikelike axis of each cone remains sitting upright in the upper crown for more than a year.

Cones of Pacific silver fir turn from green to deep purple when they ripen in late August. They appear similar to those of subalpine fir, but are larger (3½ to 6 inches long). The only other true fir growing in these high mountain forests is noble fir, and its cones are nearly covered with papery bracts. Douglas squirrels fell the dense, heavy cones of silver fir, often cutting a branch holding several of these pitchy little barrels. One morn-ing a botanist came across some of these fresh-cut cone-bearing branches along a hiking trail. He hid a few of them under a boulder some distance away, planning to retrieve them on the return trip. But the squirrel tracked down this purloined booty and spirited it away to his own cone cache before the botanist returned that afternoon.

Not only is Pacific silver fir seed comparatively large (11,000 per pound) and thus not ordinarily transported very far by the wind, but the percentage of silver fir seeds that germinate is low and they remain viable for only a short period. Sometimes the seeds germinate in late-lingering snowpack, and when this melts away, they are left with their roots exposed atop the forest-floor duff. Moreover, seedlings of silver fir have done poorly when planted in logged areas.

Pacific silver fir has thin bark and shallow roots, and is therefore usually killed by any forest fires. Because of its heavy seed and difficulties in regeneration this species apparently requires a few centuries to re-invade large burned-over areas. Unlike its higher elevation associates, subalpine fir, mountain hemlock, and Alaska-cedar, silver fir does not regenerate vegetatively (through layering of lower branches), and must rely on its seed alone.

From the preceding discussion one might infer that Pacific silver fir leads a precarious existence. Actually, this is not the case, because it has one key advantage over its associates: silver fir is extremely tolerant of dense shade, and thus has a superior ability to regenerate beneath and eventually replace its companions in the forest. For this reason Pacific silver fir is considered the potential climax species at middle elevations in the west slope forests. However, periodic disturbances (e.g., fire, blowdowns, avalanche, insect epidemics, and logging) every few centuries keep most stands from reaching such a climax condition.

Under natural conditions silver fir seedlings can become established on moist duff, moss-covered humus, or mineral soil. The tree characteristically grows slowly, at first developing a narrow,

Pacific silver fir cone debris

symmetrical crown, but not forming as slender a spire as subalpine fir. Mature trees develop a dome-shaped crown, as well as tall slender trunks covered with smooth, ashy-gray bark covered with large chalk-colored blotches. Only the largest trunks develop a rough-textured, flaky bark. Young Pacific silver firs and other true firs, as well as Douglas-fir, have large resin-filled blisters protruding from their smooth bark. These blisters contain "Canadian balsam," which is the source of the common name "balsam fir." This substance is used commercially as a mounting material for microscope slides.

After 300 to 400 years of growth on a good site, Pacific silver firs commonly attain diameters of 3 or 4 feet and reach 150 to 200 feet in height. Maximum ages are about 500 years, but very old trees become increasingly susceptible to a variety of rotting fungi and bark beetles.

The most serious threat to silver fir at present is a defoliating insect introduced from Europe by man. This balsam woolly aphid (*Chermes piceae*) was first observed killing Pacific silver fir in southwestern Washington in 1954. Unlike most insect plagues, this one kills the fastest-growing (most vigorous) trees first. Natural control of this aphid is thought to be more promising than control by means of chemicals or the logging of infested trees. To achieve this end, foresters have imported and cultured populations of some of the parasites that keep the aphid populations in check in European fir forests.

Pacific silver fir usually grows in mixed stands with western hemlock, western redcedar, and Douglas-fir; but unlike these associates it seldom descends to low elevations. With increasing elevation those associates thin out and are replaced by mountain hemlock, Alaska-cedar, and subalpine fir. However, unlike these latter associates, Pacific silver fir rarely ascends to the upper limits of tree growth; evidently silver fir is not as frost-hardy as the timberline dwellers. For example, a snow storm and hard frost at the beginning of July 1969 killed the succulent new growth on silver fir, but caused no noticeable damage to mountain hemlock, subalpine fir, whitebark pine, or alpine larch at a timberline site in Washington's North Cascades.

Incidentally, the mention of "larch" to a West Coast logger will summon visions to him of the smooth whitish-gray trunks of Pacific silver fir, since "larch" is probably the commonest term for this tree among timbermen. The logs are excellent for wood pulp, and they are suitable for plywood as well as for lumber where strength and decay-resistance are not important. Silver fir logs develop rot rapidly if left lying more than a year on the forest floor.

Although the discovery of this species came early in the history of the Northwest, its actual existence later became shrouded in doubt. It was discovered by David Douglas in 1825 not far from Mount Hood, and was first cultivated from seed he brought back to England. Another naturalist-explorer named Jeffrey found it in 1856, but when later field investigators failed to locate it, some botanical authorities, believing that it was merely a misidentified grand fir, began to question its identity, and consequently did not include it in their tree books. Finally, in 1880, three prominent botanists who had doubted its existence (Engelmann, Sargent, and Parry) rediscovered Pacific silver fir in the mountains above Fort Hope on the Fraser River.

Because of its beautiful foliage, gardeners have long shown an interest in cultivating Pacific silver fir. It often does well when grown west of the Cascades, and in the highlands of Wales and Scotland, but elsewhere the results have frequently been disappointing. Many a horticulturist has lamented that this species is more "lovely" in the wild than in the garden.

Grand Fir

Abies grandis
Pine family (*Pinaceae*)

Grand fir grows only in the Pacific Northwest, but is wide-spread at lower elevations in this region. West of the Cascades it extends from Vancouver Island and the adjacent mainland southward to the redwood forest belt of northwestern California. Its other common name, "lowland white fir," is descriptive of its Pacific Coast occurrence, since it is usually confined to valley sites between sea level and 1000 feet elevation in British Columbia, below 2000 feet in western Washington, and below 3000 feet in western Oregon.

Unlike many other Northwest trees, grand fir becomes more abundant east of the Cascades in the moister mountain ranges of the Inland Empire. It grows from Kootenay Lake, British Columbia, south to the vicinities of Burns, Oregon and Boise, Idaho, and eastward into western Montana. Extensive forests dominated by grand fir trees 3 to 5 feet thick and 150 feet high cover the moist mountainsides in northern Idaho's Nezperce and Clearwater National Forests between elevations of 2000 and 6000 feet.

Grand fir is tolerant of shade, and is thus able to regenerate beneath, and eventually take over, stands where it is mixed with less tolerant species like Douglas-fir, western white pine, western larch, and ponderosa pine. Consequently, when it occurs with those species, it forms the potential climax. However, it is less tolerant of shade than western hemlock and western redcedar, so on sites moist enough to support those species, grand fir requires periodic disturbances (fire, logging, etc.) to maintain itself in the stand. The areas where grand fir is most abundant have 25 inches or more annual precipitation, but are slightly too

Grand fir: cone and lower foliage

dry for, or beyond the range limits of, western hemlock and western redcedar. In the next drier forest zone both west and east of the Cascades, Douglas-fir is the potential climax tree.

West of the Cascades, grand fir is most abundant in the moist lowland valleys that are used for farming, such as the lower Fraser Valley in British Columbia and numerous valleys draining into Puget Sound. Grand fir grows with Douglas-fir and Oregon white oak in the Willamette Valley. It is especially prevalent along small streams in rich alluvial soil.

Grand fir's distinctive form can readily be recognized from quite a distance. Its crown is made up of densely packed, flat branches that sweep down and then level out toward their tips. The top is narrowly dome-shaped. Open-grown trees are symmetrically limbed all the way down to the ground, their trunks hidden by the branches. Because of their fine symmetry and beautiful foliage at least two communities on Puget Sound (Silverdale and Tracyton) maintain living grand fir Christmas trees over 100 feet tall. Grand fir makes a nice home-sized Christmas tree, too, but it has limited use commercially for that purpose because its stiff, horizontal branches do not allow it to be packed economically.

Grand fir is easy to identify at close range. Its lower boughs have long flat needles (the longer ones being 1½ to 2¼ inches) that spread in two regular, comb-like rows from opposite sides of the twig. These flat branches are shiny, dark green above, and whitish on the under side. Grand fir needles are blunt at the tip and longer than those of any other native conifer except the pines, whose needles grow in clusters.

People seldom see grand fir cones up close because they are borne in small quantities only at the top of the tree. They are barrel-shaped, 2½ to 4¼ inches long and sit erect on the upper-most branches. Although they resemble cones of Pacific silver fir and subalpine fir in not being covered with papery bracts, they are distinct in remaining green or at least greenish purple at maturity, when they begin to disintegrate on the tree.

Grand fir's winged seeds are of medium weight (averaging 23,000 per pound) and can be dispersed up to a few hundred feet from the tree by a brisk wind. The number of seeds pro-duced annually per acre is low compared to western hemlock and Douglas-fir, and only a small percentage of these germinate suc-cessfully. However, those grand firs that do overcome these and other difficulties in getting established become tough competi-tors for growing room in the forest. Grand fir saplings are capa-ble of surviving under shady conditions and growing very slowly for decades until large trees die, creating openings that allow some of the saplings to grow faster and take over the vacant space.

On the other hand, where grand fir can get established on a burned or cleared site, it is capable of growing very rapidly. In excellent sites on Vancouver Island, grand fir was found to grow as much as 3 feet per year, with one exceptional tree attaining 140 feet at an age of only 50 years. In valleys west of the Cas-cades grand fir is second only to Douglas-fir in its potential for rapid growth. In northern Idaho grand fir is second only to western white pine in this respect.

Such accelerated growth is remarkable for a shade-tolerant tree. Tolerant or climax species usually grow much more slowly than the pioneer or "seral" species (like coastal Douglas-fir or lodgepole pine) whose survival strategy depends more upon get-ting established rapidly after a disturbance.

Another interesting growth characteristic of grand fir is its propensity for "epicormic branching." That is, trees in the dense forest whose lower branches have been shaded out and died, are able to produce large amounts of new lower branches if light and space suddenly becomes available. Sometimes this epicormic foliage exceeds the quantity found in the original crown.

Grand firs 5 feet thick and 200 feet tall are encountered fairly often in old-growth forests west of the Cascades as well as in northern Idaho. Large trees commonly develop forked tops as a result of two more side branches growing erect after the original growing tip is killed by lightning, storms, insects, or other forces of Nature.

This species is not long-lived, and becomes very susceptible to a number of rotting fungi and insects; 250 to 300 years is considered to be the maximum. Dead branch stubs, or scrapes from falling trees provide a point of entry for fungi partially because this species and other true firs do not exude pitch over wounds (like pines) nor do they contain decay-inhibiting properties in their wood (like redcedar, redwood, juniper). One study revealed that rot readily entered 90 percent of the grand firs that were scraped during a logging operation.

East of the Cascade Crest this problem is more serious because of the ubiquitousness of the trunk-rotting Indian paint fungus (*Echinodontium tinctorium*). The presence of Indian paint fungus can be verified by sighting its conks or fruiting-bodies. These large "brackets" or hoof-shaped conks are attached to the trunk, often high above ground. Closer inspection will distinguish this conk from those of other rotting fungi, since its lower surface is made up of grayish spines. The interior of the conk is rust-red and was used by Indians as a pigment.

The presence of Indian paint conks indicates that the tree is rotten. Some ostensibly healthy looking grand fir stands are essentially worthless for timber because they are so badly infected with this and other fungi. Interestingly, this particular fungus is very limited west of the Cascades, perhaps because the cooler summers there do not favor it.

Mature grand firs have dark-gray, ridged bark about 2 inches thick that provides some protection against low-intensity forest fires, but rot often enters the fire scars on surviving trees. Large, rotten grand firs are often saturated with water, which freezes during sub-zero weather (east of the Cascade Crest), and produces conspicuous frost cracks running down the trunks. The roots generally extend deep and also stretch out a considerable distance horizontally; thus grand firs are well anchored and are wind-firm when not rotten.

Grand fir wood is light in weight, and not particularly strong.

Like that of other true firs, it is very good for pulping and is suitable for a number of light-duty uses. Rotten old grand firs are often among the largest trees to be found in the mountains east of the Cascade Divide, and there they undoubtedly prove quite valuable for wildlife. Such veteran firs provide excellent nesting and feeding sites for woodpeckers and a variety of other birds and for squirrels. The hollowed trunks are used as denning sites by various small mammals and by bears, and human campers have also found large, spreading grand firs to be a hospitable place for sitting out a downpour, since the flat, downswept boughs shed water like a tent. Of course there could be drawbacks to camping beneath a bear-den tree!

Grand fir was discovered by David Douglas and was first cultivated in 1830 from seeds he took back to Great Britain. It is a beautiful tree when cultivated west of the Cascades or in other moist parts of the Pacific Northwest, but is sometimes confused both in cultivation and in the wild with the ecologically similar white fir (*Abies concolor*), native to southern Oregon and California. Closer inspection should eliminate any confusion since white fir has gray-bluish needles, or at least some waxy bands of this color on the upper surface; in contrast, grand fir needles are shiny dark green above. White fir needles may be somewhat two-ranked, but do not form flattened branches like those of grand fir. A significant exception to this marked difference between grand fir and white fir occurs in parts of southwestern and eastern Oregon and west-central Idaho, where intermediate forms, quite possibly the result of natural hybridization, are often found. However, these intermediates will generally key more closely to grand fir than to white fir.

Subalpine Fir

Abies lasiocarpa
Pine family (*Pinaceae*)

Subalpine fir adds the crowning touch to high-country splendor in the Pacific Northwest. Clusters of these trees, shaped like narrow cathedral spires, grow amidst the meadows at timberline on Mount Rainier, at Manning Provincial Park, Mount Hood, and at hundreds of other locations all across the high mountains.

Subalpine fir is by far the most widespread true fir (*Abies*) in western North America. It can be found all the way from Yukon Territory and isolated stands in the Alaska Panhandle, south through the Rockies to New Mexico and Arizona, and southward along the Pacific Coast ranges to southern Oregon. This species becomes most abundant near upper timberline, and commonly dwells between elevations of 4000 and 7000 feet from the Cascade Divide westward. However, in the southern Rocky Mountains it finds suitable habitats only between 9500 and 11,500 feet in elevation.

Some readers are undoubtedly wondering how this species relates to the tree "alpine fir" that they have heard about. This is a more ecologically significant question than one might suspect. It so happens that "alpine fir" and subalpine fir are one and the same species, and that the latter name has become accepted by foresters because it is a more accurate description of *Abies lasiocarpa*. "Alpine" in a strict botanical or ecological sense applies to the tundra zone above timberline. Although groves of this species do form the lower boundary of the alpine zone, the tree also extends to substantially lower elevations; it grows in rocky sites, avalanche swaths, and along narrow canyon bottoms (where cold-air accumulates) down to 2500 feet in western Washington. It would probably be more widespread at these middle elevations west of the Cascade Crest except that it can not

compete well in the dense forests composed of Pacific silver fir, western hemlock, and western redcedar which dominate most sites.

In contrast, on the drier mountains east of the Cascade Divide and in parts of the Northern Rockies where the latter species are absent or scarce, subalpine fir is among the most shade-tolerant of all trees, commonly forming the potential climax at middle and sometimes even at relatively low elevations; it is, for instance, the climax species in several cool, lowland valleys (3200 to 4500 feet) west of the Continental Divide in Montana.

Furthermore, subalpine fir tolerates a broad range of moisture conditions. Although it tends to lose ground to its maritime mountain associates, mountain hemlock and Alaska-cedar, in the wettest west-side high-country areas, such as in the mountains of Vancouver Island, the British Columbia Coast Range, and on Mount Baker, it is still a major dominant at timberline in some areas that receive 150 or more inches of annual precipitation, such as in the Olympic Mountains. From this extreme, subalpine fir extends eastward to dry mountains in the rain shadow of the North Cascades, where it grows on cool sites that receive as little as 25 inches of annual precipitation. East of the Cascade Crest it grows with a broad range of associates, including whitebark pine and alpine larch at the highest elevations, Engelmann spruce in relatively moist sites, and lodgepole pine, western larch, Douglas-fir, western white pine, grand fir, and even ponderosa pine in some areas at middle elevations.

Subalpine fir has a shape well suited for survival in snowy habitats: the branches are extremely stiff (apparently a disadvantage for a timberline tree) but exceedingly tough, and since they are so short and densely packed together, the resulting crown is like an A-frame snow roof.

Unlike most other forest trees, subalpine fir is characteristically limbed to the ground, and at timberline the lower branches often form long and luxuriant "skirts." They lie sheltered in the snowpack throughout the long winter and are thus protected from damaging blizzards and immense loads of clinging ice and snow. When these lower boughs become compressed against the moist, duff-covered ground they often take root, and then send up a vertical leader. This vegetative reproduction is termed "layering," and subalpine fir often layers extensively at timberline.

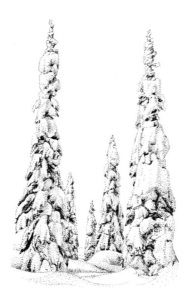

Snow-laden subalpine fir

Layering is one reason that subalpine firs so often grow in clusters at timberline. When one tree overcomes the great difficulties of becoming established in this severe climate, its lower branches may take root, then gradually grow upward to form a circle of new trunks. Eventually the mother tree in the middle of such a grove will die and rot away, leaving a hollow center in the cluster, which is then called a "timber atoll." Subalpine fir also yields sizable seed crops, but germination and especially survival of new trees is a precarious proposition at timberline.

In addition to its narrow, needle-pointed crown, subalpine fir has other features that aid in identification. Its bark is smooth (except for resin blisters) and light gray, although on older trunks it develops shallow vertical cracks. In late summer clusters of cylindrical cones (2½ to 4 inches long) can readily be seen sitting upright on short, rigid boughs; set against the deep blue mountain sky, the tree top may resemble a colorful candelabrum. Viewed more closely, as is often possible on the stunted trees at timberline, these cones are strikingly beautiful, purple, and often covered with an "icing" of pitch that sparkles in the sunlight. This is a look-but-don't-touch beauty, however, as any

High elevation subalpine fir: clusters (timber atoll) and exposed specimens

one who has gotten sticky balsam pitch on his hands can attest!

Subalpine fir's foliage is a rather deep green, and the needles have fine white bands on all sides. These are rows of microscopic pores called stomates that allow the leaves to take in carbon dioxide (for photosynthesis) and to give off oxygen; they also serve as avenues for transpiration of water vapor from the tree. The blunt needles are nearly an inch long and grow out from all sides of the twig, making a brush-like bough.

Although this is the "typical" appearance, many a forestry or botany student has encountered subalpine fir foliage (especially on saplings or trees in dense forests) that looks for all the world like Douglas-fir. This is where knowledge of several characteristics pays off in identification: buds of subalpine fir are blunt, while Douglas-fir buds are sharp-pointed, and even at the sapling stage, subalpine fir bark does not resemble the bacon-like bark described for Douglas-fir. Also, cones provide a positive identification for pole-size or larger Douglas-firs.

Every 2 to 4 years subalpine fir produces ample cone crops, and the lightweight seeds (37,000 per pound) have relatively high viability in a variety of shade and soil or duff conditions.

Like many climax species, however, subalpine fir is slow growing. Even in relatively moderate forest sites, trees 5 or 6 inches
thick are often 100 or more years of age. When logging or an
intense fire clears off a forest site east of the Cascade Crest,
subalpine fir may seed in as rapidly as Douglas-fir, lodgepole
pine, and western larch, but these pioneer or "seral" species will
rapidly attain dominance. Then, over the decades, subalpine fir
perseveres and increases in the forest understory, and without
further disturbance for a few centuries it will gradually replace
the pioneer species.

Subalpine fir's superior ability to regenerate under a variety of
conditions is crucial to its success, since it has many weaknesses
and is generally short-lived, seldom surviving more than 250
years. Its thin, resinous bark and habit of retaining combustible
lower limbs almost assures its destruction in even a relatively
low-intensity forest fire. Explorers Lewis and Clark described
how the Nez Perce Indians would set fire to individual trees in
the Bitterroot Mountains as sort of a fireworks display; these
were very likely subalpine firs.

The trunk is very brittle and susceptible to rot. A native insect
called western budworm (*Choristoneura fumiferana*) has defoliated and killed large quantities of subalpine fir in some areas

Subalpine fir

east of the Cascades. Three species of snow molds sometimes cover nearly the entire crown of small trees, whose foliage remains trapped in wet snowpack well into summer. (Snow mold imparts a matted, blackish, moribund appearance to limbs emerging from the snowpack.)

Subalpine fir also has climatic rigors to endure. Deep snowpack may not melt away until mid-summer. Heavy glaze ice coupled with hurricane winds frequently breaks off the trunks. Mid-summer frost and snow storms often cause cone crops to abort and kill succulent new growth. Winter temperatures sometimes plummet to −50° F. (−46° C.) or colder in stands east of the Cascades, and this may follow close on the heels of balmy above-freezing weather. Severe fluctuations in temperature accompanied by high winds can cause "winter drought" damage or desication of exposed foliage.

This orange-colored drought-killed foliage is most prevalent on the shrub-like, "krummholz" firs that cling to the loftiest ridges. The height attained by such krummholz often corresponds to the typical depth of the winter snowpack. Shoots that protrude through this protective blanket are ice-blasted and desicated, thus they are kept pruned back to the snowpack level.

Mature subalpine firs 200 years old may be anywhere from one to 140 feet tall. The former is typical of alpine scrub, growing in the lee of a boulder in the tundra zone; the latter dimension applies to trees along lower-elevation stream courses. Still, this is the smallest of the six major species of true firs inhabiting western North America.

In 1964 some hikers ran across an immense tree in a high basin in Olympic National Park. In addition to its gigantic size, this tree was remarkable because it had a wooden door neatly affixed to the base of its great bole. Investigation revealed that this was not an elf's house. Instead, some enterprising mountaineer had sealed off a large cavity in the trunk in order to use it as a cache cabin. More surprising was the fact that this huge tree was a living subalpine fir. (This largest known subalpine fir is nearly 7 feet thick and 129 feet tall.)

Dense thickets of subalpine firs with their stiff, often dead, lower limbs are inhospitable when they lie in the route of a cross-country hiker, but they are sought out by many species of wildlife, including deer and mountain goats, for protection from predators, hunters, and storms. These nearly impenetrable thickets seem to be a favorite hideaway for porcupines.

The wood of this tree is light in color and among the lightest of all western conifers in weight (21 pounds per cubic foot when dry). Because of the limby character of the tree, the wood is invariably knotty. Subalpine firs yield small logs, often having heart rot or other defects; nevertheless, it is useful for wood pulp, although it is seldom logged to any extent west of the Cascade Crest because it is restricted to such high elevations there.

Explorers Lewis and Clark were the first white men to describe this species, when they encountered it in the Bitterroot Mountains in 1805. It is a favorite of horticulturists because of its spire-shaped form and brush-like foliage. Strangely, despite its natural hardiness, subalpine fir is reported to suffer winter injury when planted in certain parts of New England. Perhaps the climate there does not consistently provide a snowpack sufficient for insulating the saplings from temperature extremes.

Noble Fir

Abies procera
Pine family *(Pinaceae)*

Noble fir is such a fine timber tree that early lumbermen marketed it as "Oregon larch," because "firs" *(Abies)* had little value in the timber trade in those days. (At least two "Larch Mountains" in the Cascades were so named because of their towering stands of noble fir.) However, this particular fir warranted a worthier name because it has magnificent clear trunks made of relatively strong but lightweight wood.

Noble fir is intolerant of shade, but grows mixed with shade-tolerant species in dense stands; consequently its lower limbs soon die and drop off, leaving a clear, pillar-like trunk. One 254-foot specimen measured 5 feet in diameter at its base and was still 3 feet thick at a point 160 feet above the ground. Its lowermost limb (176 feet off the ground) would have stretched out above a 17-story building. Although not a massive tree by Northwest standards, this specimen yielded over 18,000 board feet of high-grade lumber. Noble fir does, however, surpass all other of the world's 40 species of true fir in size; the largest known noble fir (9 feet thick and 278 feet tall) grows in the Gifford Pinchot National Forest in southwestern Washington.

Noble fir, like Pacific silver fir, grows at middle elevations (mostly between 2500 and 5000 feet) in the mountains of western Washington and western Oregon. It inhabits the Cascades from Stevens Pass east of Seattle southward to Crater Lake National Park, where it is abundant between elevations of 5500 and 8000 feet. It also grows in the Siskiyous, reaching southward barely into California, where it intergrades extensively with a closely related species known as red fir *(Abies magnifica)*.

Noble fir was once thought to grow farther north, on Mount

Baker and on the Soleduck River in the Olympics, but those early reports have never been confirmed. It does occupy the Willapa Hills of southwestern Washington as well as the higher peaks of the Oregon Coast Range, mostly above 2000 feet elevation (for instance Saddle Mountain near Astoria and Marys Peak west of Corvallis). Visitors can readily find it growing in the middle to upper elevation forests (but below timberline) on Mount Rainier and Mount Hood.

Some large noble firs still growing on the south slope of Mount Hood were used by pioneers in the mid-1800s to control the descent of their wagons down a steep hill on the Barlow Road. This braking action was accomplished by tying a rawhide rope to the back of the wagon and wrapping it around the tree trunk (at the top of the hill), then allowing it to feed out slowly as the wagon descended. Some of the rope-burned noble fir "snub trees" can be seen on Laurel Hill about 5 miles east of Rhododendron on the south side of the Mount Hood Loop Highway (U.S. 26).

Noble fir seems to require a cool, moist habitat. On these sites average annual precipitation ranges from about 70 to 120 inches, and summer temperatures rarely exceed 85° F. (29° C.). It also grows surprisingly well on the rockiest soils if they remain moist throughout the summer. Soil moisture is especially critical for regeneration because the roots of noble fir seedlings grow slowly.

Even under good conditions in natural stands noble fir seedlings require 3 to 4 years to reach a foot in height, and about 10 years to grow 4 feet. Such slow growth would certainly be a critical disadvantage for a West Coast tree that is intolerant of shade; however, after about 10 years, noble fir ascends rapidly toward the sky, keeping even with or ahead of all its associates.

At middle elevations it grows mixed with equally tall Douglas-fir and smaller western hemlock. At higher altitudes Pacific silver fir, mountain hemlock, and subalpine fir become its principal associates. All of these except Douglas-fir are shade tolerant. Consequently, noble fir depends on occasional disturbances to create openings and allow it to regenerate.

This species has the advantage of being long-lived for a true fir (probably 600 to 700 years maximum), so the fire, logging, or blowdowns it requires for self-replacement need not occur very often. Furthermore it resists damage by insects and diseases more than other true firs or western hemlock, and is also relatively wind-firm and resists breaking under heavy snow loads. Although its thin bark affords little protection against forest fire, these occur very infrequently in these moist mountain sites.

Noble fir has several distinctive features that aid in identification. Its needles are stiff, closely crowded, and upturned to form a dense brush-like growth on the upper side of the twig. In contrast, the under surface of the branchlet has a flat, combed appearance. The foliage ranges from a pale, almost silvery color to deep bluish-green; however its needles contrast with those of other true firs in havings two whitish bands (made up of thousands of microscopic pores called stomates) on their upper as well as their lower surfaces. (Subalpine fir has one broad band above and two below, while Pacific silver and grand firs have only the two lower bands.)

Unlike other true firs, noble fir's needles (even on lower branches) are plump rather than being noticeably flattened in cross-section. Young trees have a beautiful pyramidal crown which, combined with the dense brush-like foliage, makes them highly prized for Christmas trees and landscaping.

Since noble fir foliage is often far out of reach in old-growth stands, other characteristics are needed for identification. The crown of mature trees is quite small (being confined to the top one-third of trees in dense stands), open, dome-shaped, and made up of relatively short, stiff, horizontal branches. The towering trunk of mature trees is covered with ashy-brown bark divided by vertical seams into flat narrow ridges These ridges of bark are broken into long plates that flake off readily to reveal the reddish inner bark.

Identification will prove easy if cones can be found. Sometimes they can be observed in the tree tops with binoculars, or discovered on the ground where squirrels have felled them unshattered. Noble fir cones are erect, barrel-shaped, and larger than those of other Northwest firs — 4½ to 7 inches long and 2½ inches thick. (Cultivated trees bear still larger cones.) But more important for identification, the noble fir cones have an ornate, "shingled" surface covered with papery bracts that extend out and down from between the cone scales. Even after the cones have disintegrated, the scales with their longer, protruding bract

Noble fir

still attached, can be found lying on the forest floor.

These interesting cones are light green in mid-summer, but become tan by early autumn, when they dry out and disintegrate, spreading seeds far into the winds. Noble fir's winged seeds are moderately heavy (14,600 per pound), but experiments have shown that a light breeze will carry them more than a quarter of a mile from the tree top. The seeds remain viable only one year, and therefore must germinate the following spring. Under favorable conditions, noble fir and Douglas-fir often seed in quickly to re-establish a stand on sizeable clearcuts or burned areas.

Horticulturists and foresters in Great Britain have been interested in noble fir ever since their visting naturalist David Douglas first discovered this towering Northwest tree in 1825 and brought back seed for cultivation. Noble fir has become a productive timber species in forest plantations in moister parts of the British Isles. Some cultivated trees there have grown to more than 150 feet tall. Even the Royal Air Force has had a stake in noble fir; its light, strong wood was reportedly used for the frames of their Mosquito bombers during World War II.

Incense-cedar

Calocedrus decurrens
Cypress family *(Cupressaceae)*

To Northwesterners who tend to think of "cedars" as trees that grow in wet places, incense-cedar may seem an anomaly. Although it is a large tree with fluted butt and lacy foliage, much like our wet-site "cedars," incense-cedar can survive on even drier sites than Douglas-fir. It is second only to ponderosa pine and junipers in drought tolerance. Incense-cedar inhabits areas on the east slope of the Oregon Cascades that receive as little as 15 inches of annual precipitation. Southward, in California this tree joins ponderosa pine in forming the lower limits of coniferous forest amidst the hot chaparral-covered foothills.

Incense-cedar is most abundant in the lower mountain forests of California and southwestern Oregon, but it extends northward in diminishing numbers along the Cascades to the southeastern slopes of Mount Hood. It also inhabits some of the semi-arid mountains east of Bend in central Oregon. Incense-cedar does not occur in the Coast Range north of Coos Bay.

Young incense-cedars can be recognized from quite a distance by their dense symmetrical crowns, which form perfect pyramids. They can readily be sighted along the Wapinita Cutoff (State Highway 216) on the east slope of the Cascades south of Mount Hood. Travelers heading east on this route can first see incense-cedars near Bear Springs, and will then find them scattered for 20 miles along the route leading into increasingly desert-like conditions. West of the Cascades, incense-cedars dot the rolling hillsides and old pastures along Interstate 5 south of Cottage Grove, Oregon. The species also grows at lower elevations in Crater Lake National Park.

Older incense-cedars can also be distinguished by swollen bases supporting rapidly tapering trunks covered with deeply furrowed orange-brown bark. Such old-growth veterans often have large "catfaces" or blackened wounds caused by forest fires. Their crowns are open and irregular, often with scattered, clumpy branches called "witches brooms" that result from long-term infection by the parasitic mistletoe plant *(Phoradendron juniperinum)*. Some mistletoe infections in living incense-cedars are estimated to date back 400 years.

Naturalist John Muir described incense-cedar as a tree that in its prime is densely thatched with beautiful fern-like plumes, thus shedding rain and snow, and making a fine shelter. Muir also recounted that, as the tree gets older it is likely to put out large special branches from the upper crown. These form "big, stubborn elbows, and then shoot up parallel with the axis. Very old trees are usually dead at the top, the main axis protruding above ample masses of green plumes, gray and lichen-covered, and drilled full of acorn holes by the woodpeckers." (With reference to acorns, incense-cedar often grows with Oregon white oak and California black oak in southern Oregon and California.)

Incense-cedar foliage is also quite distinctive. Its boughs are made up of scale-like leaves pressed tightly against the twigs. Some of these scaly leaves are quite long (up to ½ inch). Incense-cedar has flattened branchlets that terminate in fan-like sprays. Copious crops of tiny pollen-bearing flowers ripen at an unusual time of year, tinging the incense-cedar with golden yellow in winter and early spring.

Female or seed-bearing cones often cover these trees, and could hardly be confused with fruits of any other species. At first they resemble little green urns an inch long. Later, they turn brown and the two large scales bend back from the axis of the cone in a manner resembling a duck's bill, wide-open with the tongue extended straight out. Although the seeds are moderately heavy (averaging 15,000 per pound) each has a large wing and can be buoyed quite a distance by the wind.

In summer following a good seed year, curious little seedlings can be found on the forest floor. These new incense-cedars, just a few inches high, have several types of leaves: a pair of inch-long needle-like seed-leaves (cotyledons) at the base, shorter needles giving way to prickly awls farther up the stem, then tiny scale-like leaves near the tip of the first year's shoots.

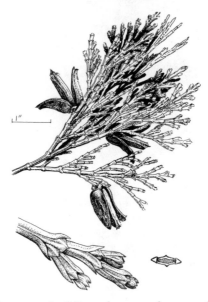

Incense-cedar foliage: close-up and cross-section

Incense-cedars can regenerate under a wide range of light intensities on mineral soil or duff; often its seedlings grow up beneath mountain shrubs. It is relatively tolerant of shade (more so than the Douglas-fir, ponderosa pine, and sugar pine with which it commonly grows on drier sites) so it is a "climax" species in those situations. However, in the northern Oregon Cascades incense-cedar typically grows as a minor component of stands having western hemlock, western redcedar, and grand fir, all of which are more shade-tolerant than it is. Incense-cedar needs an occasional disturbance to survive in those stands.

Incense-cedar's thick basal bark (up to 6 inches on old trees) protects it from ground fires, an advantage over western hemlock, western redcedar, and grand fir. However, fire commonly leaves large scars on the surviving trees, and these become ports of entry for a dry rot *(Polyporus amarus)* that eventually honeycombs the wood with small cavities. A very high percentage of old-growth incense-cedars in southern Oregon and California are fire-scarred and are riddled with this dry pocket rot. This seems ironic, considering that incense-cedar (heartwood) lumber is highly resistant to decay.

Seedlings of incense-cedar grow more slowly than those of its common associates, ponderosa and sugar pine. In one study incense-cedar roots grew only 12 inches the first year, while pine roots reached down 20 inches. Unlike the pines, however, incense-cedar can successfully reproduce in conifer-needle litter. Incense-cedar develops even more slowly above the ground, often attaining only 6 inches in height after 3 to 5 years. On especially dry sites or beneath a dense forest canopy, saplings often reach only 3 feet in height in 30 years. Nevertheless, even under these austere conditions they can eke out an existence and will grow faster if an opening arises in the stand.

Under favorable conditions, incense-cedars in Oregon attain diameters of 3 to 4 feet and heights of 140 feet during their 500-year life-span. They often grow larger than this in southwestern Oregon and California.

The common name incense-cedar is indeed appropriate for this tree, which is one of several species used for making fragrant, "mothproof" cedar chests, and whose leaves give off a pungent aromatic odor when crushed. The wood is soft, lightweight and very rot-resistant. It is particularly useful for fence posts and shingles, and is the world's leading pencil wood.

Incense-cedar is hyphenated for the same reason as is Douglas-fir: like Alaska-cedar (a false-cypress) or western redcedar (an arborvitae), it is not really a cedar. (The eastern North American redcedar is really a juniper. In fact, the only true cedars (genus *Cedrus*) in the world — cedar of Lebanon, deodar, and Atlas cedars — are native to the eastern Mediterranean, northern Africa, and the Himalayas, respectively. They have needle-like leaves and do not resemble any of the trees we call "cedar.")

Until rather recently botanists classified incense-cedar as a member of the diverse genus *Libocedrus*, which was cited as the only genus of conifers encircling the Pacific Ocean — its other species growing in South America, New Zealand, New Caledonia, New Guinea, southern China, and Taiwan. However, detailed investigations of these trees showed that cones of the three species growing north of the Equator differ markedly in structure from the others. Thus our incense-cedar and two Oriental species were reclassified in the new genus, *Calocedrus*, meaning "beautiful cedar." (Older books use *Libocedrus* for incense-cedar;

Flora of the Pacific Northwest, by Hitchcock and Cronquist has adopted *Calocedrus*.) Like incense-cedar, the other species of *Calocedrus* are important timber trees having rot-resistant wood. Large Chinese *Calocedrus* trees which were buried in past geologic ages have been perfectly preserved and are reportedly "mined" and sawn into coffin stock.

Incense-cedar is a handsome tree in cultivation and is successful in a wide range of climates, including even southern New England. It forms a dense, narrow pyramidal crown and grows as much as 2 feet per year after becoming established.

Western Redcedar

Thuja plicata
Cypress family *(Cupressaceae)*

Western redcedar was the most valuable tree known to Indians of the Northwest Coast, providing materials for their shelters, clothing, and even for the dugout canoes and fishing nets they used in obtaining food. The wood of this common Northwest tree is still highly valued for shelter, being the major source of shingles, shakes, and boards for untreated (natural finish) exterior siding in North America. Hand-split western redcedar shakes sell for several times the price of asphalt shingles, but will last 100 years on a roof. Demand for western redcedar is so great that partially rotten butt-sections left in logging slash command a good price, and "cedar poaching" of scattered live trees or even of marketable logging slash is a thriving illicit trade!

This prized tree grows along the Pacific Coast from the southern part of the Alaska Panhandle through British Columbia, western Washington, and western Oregon, barely reaching into the coastal redwood forest of extreme northern California. It grows mainly between sea level and 3500 feet elevation in the coastal Northwest, but reaches about 4500 feet in southwestern Oregon. It also occupies the moistest parts of the Rocky Mountain System in southeastern British Columbia, northeastern Washington, northern Idaho, and northwestern Montana, usually below 5000 feet elevation. Its range here is generally similar to that of western white pine, western hemlock, and grand fir.

Western redcedar is characteristically a tree of moist habitats. It grows best in areas of definite maritime climate with cool, cloudy summers and wet, mild winters. It is usually found where annual precipitation averages well over 30 inches, and reaches optimum development in valleys receiving from 60 to 120 inches

of rainfall. In drier areas west of the Cascades, western redcedar becomes abundant only on wet sites such as in ravines, along streams, or on poorly drained bottomlands. Near its range limits in the drier mountains east of the Cascade Crest, western redcedar grows almost exclusively in narrow canyons, where its roots are irrigated all summer by a mountain stream.

This species thrives on mucky soils, often forming nearly pure groves of giant trees with fluted butts accompanied by a luxuriant undergrowth of ferns, skunk cabbage *(Lysichitum americanum)*, or devils club *(Oplopanax horridum)*. The latter, a shrub with stems and large leaves armed with sharp spines, is known only too well to hikers.

Western redcedars have conical trunks, tapering rapidly from their heavily buttressed bases, and are anchored by shallow, widely spreading root systems. At maturity they become massive trees with broad crowns made up of spreading, drooping branches that turn up at their tips. Except when densely crowded, this species retains its lower limbs. Young trees have a drooping, whip-like leader (terminal shoot), but old trees often develop "spike tops" with dead, bleached fork-like arms poking up into the damp air.

On better sites west of the Cascades, old-growth western redcedars often attain basal diameters of 8 to 10 feet and heights of 200 feet; they grow nearly as large in moist stream bottom sites in the Rockies. The largest known western redcedars are believed to be about 1000 years old, and in that time have reached phenomenal proportions. Two trees growing in the western part of Olympic National Park are each over 20 feet in diameter, although both their tops have snapped off 120 to 130 above the ground. In 1974 a tree nearly 19 feet thick and 178 feet tall was discovered growing on State land near the town of Forks on the Olympic Peninsula. Although its market value is estimated at $20,000, this giant has been spared from the logger's axe.

The boles of these great trees are distinguished not only by their size and shape, but by a thin layer of stringy fibrous bark that readily peels off in long narrow strips. Northwest Coast Indians made their principal fiber from this bark, shredding the inner layer so finely that it could be used for diapers and cradle padding. They also wove it into fishing nets and sails for their dugout canoes, and some tribes used the bark for making clothing and blankets. Slabs or sheets of this bark are still utilized as a roofing material for sheds.

The foilage of western redcedar is also distinctive, consisting of flat lacy sprays made up of tiny scale-like leaves mostly about ⅛ inch long. Redcedar boughs give off a pleasant aromatic smell. The fern-like sprays droop gracefully from the main branches and are decorated with small leather-brown oval cones (½ to ¾ inch long) which ripen in one season. They sit erect on the foliage sprays, showing up like small dried flowers in a

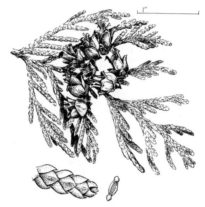

Western redcedar foliage: close-up and cross-section

winter bouquet. These cones bear seeds so small (averaging 400,000 per pound) that rodents seldom bother to eat them. Although these seeds have relatively small wings and are not carried more than about 400 feet from the parent tree, western redcedar is a prodigious seed producer, second only to western hemlock, and typical "seed rains" have been measured as a few million per acre each year in mixed stands containing this species.

Along the coast, the seeds germinate in either fall or spring, but in spite of surprisingly high germination rates for such a minute embryo, very few seedlings survive. Fungi, birds, insects, strong sunlight (lethal heating), surface soil drought, and smothering by fallen leaves of deciduous shrubs take a heavy toll. Partial sunlight is considered most advantageous to survival. Western redcedar also reproduces vegetatively to a limited extent through root systems which develop on lower limbs that touch the ground as well as on the prostrate trunks of wind-thrown trees.

Western redcedar is more tolerant of shade than any of its principal associates, excepting western hemlock. Because of its greater size and longevity, it remains as a member of undis-turbed stands indefinitely, even when growing with western hemlock, but it seldom dominates forest sites other than in very wet places where hemlock and other species do poorly. After hemlock, its principal associates west of the Cascades are Douglas-fir and Sitka spruce. In the inland forests it grows primarily with western hemlock, grand fir, western larch, west-ern white pine, and Engelmann spruce.

Another common name for this species is "giant arborvitae" ("tree of life"). The only other *Thuja* (arborvitae) in North America is the northern whitecedar, *Thuja occidentalis,* native to the northeastern United States and eastern Canada. The name "redcedar" is confusing since it is also applied to an east-ern species of juniper *(Juniperus virginiana);* however "western redcedar" is firmly entrenched in forestry and lumbering nomenclature.

Western redcedar is certainly prized in the lumber industry despite the fact that its wood is very light in weight, soft, weak, and brittle. Its most valuable attributes are resistance to decay and a straight grain that allows it to be split easily into shakes and fence posts. Rough cut western redcedar siding and paneling has an attractive orange-brown color as well as a frag-rant odor and needs no stain or other finish when used either outside or inside. The heartwood owes its lengendary decay-resistance to a natural fungicide.

The wood is also easy to carve and work with tools; hence its exclusive use by Northwest Indians for their large totem poles and dugout canoes, which were initially hollowed out by fire and then finished with the aid of stone implements. Redcedar dug-outs were reportedly as much as 60 feet long and 8 feet across, fitted with masts and a sail, and capable of carrying 30 to 40 people.

White men made early use of western redcedar for boats. Lewis and Clark were introduced to this tree by their Nez Perce guides while journeying westward down the Clearwater River in what is now northern Idaho; near the present site of Orofino, the party hollowed out western redcedar logs to make four large pirogues (dugouts) that would transport them downstream to the Pacific.

In about 1900, Captain J. C. Voss purchased a 38-foot redcedar dugout canoe from Vancouver Island Indians. He added a cabin and three masts, and sailed the canoe around the world. This craft is now kept on display at Thunderbird Park in Victoria.

Northwest Indians also used western redcedar for many medicinal and ritualistic purposes. Early settlers and modern Northwesterners alike have found it outstanding for the construction of log houses that easily last a century in the dampest climate. Many a cold, wet explorer or modern camper has been thankful to find a fallen western redcedar and the sure-fire kindling that it provides.

Still other uses of this species include landscaping. It is a handsome tree in cultivation, limbed to the ground with long, sweeping boughs. Also, unlike many conifers, it sprouts new foliage along the trunk (epicormic branches) and thus responds well to pruning, developing into attractive, full-bodied hedges.

Various creatures of the forest find cozy dwellings inside large hollow cavities with narrow entrances between the root buttresses of old-growth western redcedars. Bears, raccoons, skunks, and other animals find these dry, secluded caverns make fine dens — with cedar paneling inside and out!

In 1898 Thomas Stringham, an imaginative settler in the Elwha Valley west of Port Angeles, Washington, made a family home and U.S. post office out of a huge western redcedar stump on his property. Decay and ancient forest fires had hollowed out the tree, which had been logged to a tall stump. Mr. Stringham built only the roof — out of redcedar shakes.

A number of bole-rotting fungi are active in living western redcedars, with the yellow ring rots *(Poria spp.)* the most prominent. Nevertheless, this tree is durable in life as well as after death. Insects have a minor effect on it, snow loads inflict little damage on its supple boughs and it is relatively wind-firm despite its shallow roots. Although easily damaged or killed by fire, flames seldom sweep through the wet sites where it grows most abundantly. Still, even the arborvitae must eventually topple and be recycled into the forest floor duff and soil. When a western redcedar patriarch is finally returned to the earth, seedlings of the same species are likely to be among the first to grow on its slowly decomposing remains, thus beginning another 1000-year life cycle.

Alaska-cedar

Chamaecyparis nootkatensis
Cypress family *(Cupressaceae)*

Visitors to the high country of the Cascades and coastal ranges of the Northwest often notice an unusual "cedar" with bluish-green lace-like sprays that hang limply, giving it a weeping appearance. This Alaska-cedar, which inhabits the coastal mountain ranges from south-central Alaska to southwestern Oregon, with a few isolated groves in the Siskiyous just inside California, grows from tidewater to timberline in the northern part of its range, but south of Juneau, Alaska, it occurs at increasingly high elevations. The southernmost sea-level groves occupy the fiord country near Mount Waddington, British Columbia; however, Alaska-cedar is usually found between 2500 and 6500 feet elevation in southwestern British Columbia, western Washington, and western Oregon. It also dwells at timberline and in the alpine scrub communities.

Alaska-cedar's primary requirement for successful growth seems to be a cold, wet maritime climate in which annual precipitation exceeds 60 inches, winter snowfall accumulates to great depths, and the trees are seldom exposed to temperatures much below zero degrees F. (−18° C.). In the fog-bound coastal mountains, Alaska-cedar does not even require soil, and may form huge sprawling shrubs on rocky crags at timberline; at lower elevations it can grow on a thin mantle of wet soil on top of bedrock. It also coexists with shore pine on boggy sites near Tofino, Vancouver Island.

Alaska-cedar is one of the few Northwest conifers (along with Pacific silver fir and noble fir) that is restricted to the Pacific coast mountains and does not occur even in the wettest ranges east of the Cascades. There are a couple of interesting exceptions to this

rule: a stand of Alaska-cedar is found about 400 miles inland at Hird and Evans Lakes near Slocan Lake in southeastern British Columbia, and a 10-acre grove occupies a cool ravine at 5500-foot elevation in the Aldrich Mountains of central Oregon, about 140 miles east of the species' main distribution in the Cascades. These remarkably isolated groves are thought to be remnants of a more extensive Alaska-cedar forest that had spread across the inland mountains during the last major Ice Age, when a cooler, wetter climate prevailed.

Alaska-cedar is most abundant along mountain streams and in moist swales, but even in these sites it seldom forms pure stands. At its lowest limits it mingles with western redcedar and western hemlock. Higher up, it associates with Pacific silver fir, mountain hemlock, and subalpine fir. Although foresters consider this species to be relatively tolerant of shade, it is not as tolerant as its major associates. Moreover, Alaska-cedar grows slowly throughout life. These characteristics put it at a disadvantage in competing for growing room, and this may be why it is most common on poor, rocky soils where its competitors do not grow well.

Visitors will find Alaska-cedar in moist sites and on north-facing slopes along the roads and trails that climb beyond the 3000-foot level in the mountains of southwestern British Columbia and western Washington. It is easily spotted at Government Camp on Mount Hood, but becomes rather scarce southward in the Oregon Cascades, and does not generally form timberline there as it does farther north.

In the Olympics and mountains of Vancouver Island Alaska-cedar is very adaptable, covering a broad range of sites in the middle and higher elevation forests. Its drooping form graces many a streamside, with large trees attaining diameters of 3 to 4 feet and heights of 100 feet in their approximately 1000-year lifespan. The largest known Alaska-cedar, 10 feet thick and 113 feet tall, grows in the northeastern part of Olympic National Park.

This species also grows as wind-scoured krummholz cushions far up into the alpine tundra of the northeastern Olympics, well above the limits of other conifers. One such Alaska-cedar near the summit of Mount Angeles forms a circular mat 50 feet across and barely 3 feet high. This shrubby cushion has a hollow center, like a "timber atoll" of subalpine fir, and it may well have endured this harsh environment for 1000 years. A large living root, exposed by erosion, leads 75 feet across the steep mountainside from a similar krummholz Alaska-cedar before this anchor and life-line descends into the rocky substrate.

Krummholz of this species seems to have an advantage over the more numerous subalpine fir because its lace-like branchlets are more flexible, and less likely to be scoured off. But probably even more important is the durability of its wood, which is so rot-resistant that part of a fire-killed stand along the road to Paradise in Mount Rainier National Park was cut early in park history and used to furnish the park headquarters, even though these snags had already weathered in the soggy climate for almost 50 years.

Alaska-cedar foliage: close-up and cross-section

Alaska-cedar can be identified at quite a distance by its rather sparse branches and drooping form. The flat, fern-like sprays are made up of tiny scale-like leaves (about ⅛ inch long) that are dark bluish-green. These leaves have sharp, spreading tips; thus they seem prickly, in contrast with the smooth foliage of western redcedar. The leaves survive for two years and then turn yellow to rusty brown. Since they are not shed for another year, they often give the tree a yellowish or brownish tinge.

Alaska-cedar cones are easy to identify: they are knobby, green, and berry-like the first year, then during the second season they ripen, becoming tan and woody. Mature cones cling to the sprays long after they have shed their seeds. These cones are round (nearly ½ inch in diameter), but cut into four to six shield-like scales, separated by fissures. Each scale has a blunt, horny point.

Although the seeds are small (108,000 per pound), they have a little wing and are dispersed not very far from the parent tree. A relatively small percentage of them is viable; vegetative reproduction of Alaska-cedar is also rather limited, except in the krummholz zone.

Alaska-cedar trunks are clad in a distinctive bark that is fairly smooth and reddish on young trees, but becomes light gray with age. This mature bark is shaggy and hangs in loose rough pieces or flakes. Unlike western redcedar bark, it will not peel off in long strips.

The bark is only ½ inch thick and thus provides little protection against forest fires; however fire is not common in the cool, wet habitats where Alaska-cedar grows. The flexible, limp foliage resists damage from clinging snow-loads. Also, insects and diseases have relatively little effect on Alaska-cedar, except that ancient trees often develop heart rot which ultimately figures in their demise. This may be the longest-lived tree in the Northwest, possibly reaching 2000 years or more. A Canadian naturalist found a hollow Alaska-cedar 5½ feet thick and counted 1040 rings in its 1-foot-thick outer shell.

Part of the secret of Alaska-cedar's longevity lies in the fact that four different chemical components of its heartwood are toxic to fungi. Naturally this attribute makes the wood valuable where durability is important. But Alaska-cedar wood has other useful features, too. It is fine-grained and has good working qualities. Although light in weight, it is relatively strong and stiff and does not swell or shrink very much when soaked and dried. For these reasons it has long been prized for use in construction of small boats. However, old-time sawyers are reputed to have disliked cutting Alaska-cedar because handling the green wood somehow had a laxative effect.

Good Alaska-cedar lumber commands a high price because of its scarcity: good timber is sparse, often rather inaccessible, and takes about 200 years to reach marketable size.

Both Alaska-cedar and western redcedar were discovered in 1793 by the Scottish naturalist Archibald Menzies, who accompanied Captain George Vancouver, at Nootka Sound on the west side of Vancouver Island. The genus name *Chamaecyparis* means "false cypress" in Greek; thus the scientific name can be literally translated as "Nootka false-cypress." The false-cypress designation was chosen for this genus of trees because the cones resemble those of the cypresses *(Cupressus)*, but are smaller in size. In the timber trade, the color of the wood gave rise to the name "yellow cedar," and early foresters often called it "Alaska yellow-cedar." However, for convenience this was eventually shortened to Alaska-cedar.

Alaska-cedar prospers when cultivated in cool, moist climates, and it is hardy in southern New England. Under cultivation it becomes luxuriant and is relatively fast-growing; thus it may be unrecognizeable to those who are accustomed to seeing the rather sparsely foliated wild trees. Several Alaska-cedars in Great Britain, after a century of growth, are about 100 feet tall.

One other *Chamaecyparis* grows in western North America, and it is commonly cultivated. Moreover, it grows at lower to middle elevations along the coast of southern Oregon and northern California, so it is adjacent to our Northwest forests and worth noting. This tree is Port-Orford-cedar, *Chamaecyparis lawsoniana*. It contrasts with Alaska-cedar in being a relatively abundant, large tree of lower elevations. Also, it develops a long clear bole covered with very thick bark (6 to 10 inches), and its sprays are *not* prickly, because the leaves do not have pointed tips. The wood of Port-Orford-cedar has properties similar to Alaska-cedar and is highly valued.

Rocky Mountain Juniper and Western Juniper

Juniperus scopulorum and *Juniperus occidentalis*
Cypress family *(Cupressaceae)*

Junipers are usually squatty little trees with dense bushy foliage and tiny scale-like leaves. About a dozen species of tree-like junipers are native to the United States and Canada, and they become most abundant in the semi-arid Southwest. Two tree-like junipers extend northward into the drier reaches of the Northwest.

Rocky Mountain juniper is the most widespread juniper in western North America, occurring in all the western States except California, as well as in British Columbia and Alberta. It extends north along the Rockies into the dry valleys of western Montana and southeastern British Columbia. Small amounts of it also inhabit a number of warm, dry sites in northern Washington east of the Cascades. It can be found near the Columbia River from Chelan to Vantage, as well as in northeastern Oregon.

It may seem surprising that this dry-land tree also grows along the Northwest Coast. Nevertheless, Rocky Mountain juniper does inhabit several rocky areas in the rain-shadow of the Olympic Mountains. These junipers cling to the goat rocks on Griff Creek Trail in the Elwha River drainage of Olympic National Park. They can also be found on Fidalgo Island west of Anacortes, in much of the San Juan Islands, and in the vicinity of Victoria.

Western juniper, by contrast, is largely restricted to Oregon and California, where it forms extensive woodlands. Throughout its natural distribution, western juniper commonly forms an "advance guard" on sites too dry even for ponderosa pine. Outlying populations are reported in the vicinities of Wenatchee and Ellensburg in central Washington. Otherwise western juniper

reaches its northern limits in the hot, arid canyons near the Columbia River in southern Washington and northern Oregon. Southward, it forms pure stands east of the Cascades, alternating with big sagebrush *(Artemisia tridentata)* in dominating eastern Oregon's high desert country. Western juniper colonizes the rocky ground, but gives way to sagebrush on sites having better soil. An isolated population of western juniper is also reported near Corvallis in the Willamette Valley.

Both of these junipers become most abundant on rocky sites in the sunny interior of the Northwest. Western juniper can survive in places receiving as little as 8 inches of annual precipitation, while Rocky Mountain juniper requires only about 10 inches. Thus they are able to form an open "juniper woodland" from 15 to 20 feet tall on sites too dry for forest trees. This juniper woodland becomes a major vegetation type to the south in the Great Basin desert of eastern California, Nevada, and Utah, where it has additional species of juniper as well as pinyon pines.

Northwest junipers also grow scattered among ponderosa pine and Douglas-fir on rocky, open forest sites, but are largely restricted to inhospitably dry environments because they are unable to compete with forest trees on better sites. They can endure shade in early life, but become very intolerant of shade thereafter, and since they are so much shorter, forest trees like ponderosa pine soon overshadow them. Junipers are also rather easily killed by ground fires that have little effect on the larger ponderosa pines.

Both of these species of juniper typically form ragged, bushy little trees. The trunk of Rocky Mountain juniper, especially, is often divided into two or more stems at the base. Both species, especially western juniper, can become stout, heavy-limbed, gnarled trees over the course of many centuries. Trees of this species, on better sites in eastern Oregon, occasionally reach 4 feet in diameter and 50 feet in height. Sometimes even the junipers clinging to rocky cliffs attain great diameters after a millennium of slow growth and become picturesque "living snags" partially stripped of bark and foliage by the onslaughts of countless blizzards.

The largest known western juniper is a remarkable tree 14 feet thick and 87 feet tall growing near Sonora Pass in the Sierra Nevada of central California. This tree, the "Bennett Juniper," has been conservatively estimated to be 3000 years old. A Rocky Mountain juniper growing near Logan, Utah, is also estimated to be a 3000-year-old Methuselah; it is 6½ feet thick and 36 feet high.

The foliage of both junipers is at first confusing, since individual trees have two kinds of leaves. Mature trees have mostly tiny scale-like leaves, but juvenile shoots and especially saplings are largely covered with prickly, ½-inch-long, awl-like leaves. Once this is recognized, identification of the two species becomes easy, using the scale-like leaves, which are arranged opposite each other in pairs on the twigs of Rocky Mountain juniper, while those of western juniper are borne in whorls of three.

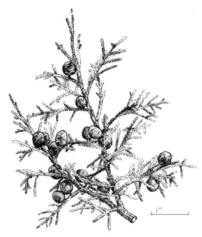

Western juniper

Juniper fruits are described as "berry-like cones." Although they are fleshy, they have the vestiges of cone scales etched into their surfaces. Regardless of the scientific classification, birds gobble these small bluish fruits, which often have a whitish waxy coating, as eagerly as if they were real berries. This is all in accordance with Nature's plan, since juniper seed does not readily germinate unless its fleshy covering is dissolved by passing through the digestive tract of birds or other animals.

Birds are apparently the principal agent of such scarification and for dissemination of juniper seed over the landscape. The rich fruits cling to the trees all winter, making an excellent food supply. Under experimental conditions one scientist found that 900 Rocky Mountain juniper fruits passed through a single Bohemian waxwing in just five hours!

Mule deer and cattle are also attracted to juniper foliage, but often only to certain individual trees. In fact, deer will raise themselves rather precariously on their hind legs to eat as much as possible of this "ice cream" foliage of certain junipers. Scientists have so far been unable to identify chemical differences in these trees, but the deer cannot be fooled. When caged deer were given branches from various juniper trees they ate only the ones from their "ice cream" trees.

Humans also have made use of juniper "berries" as the flavoring for gin. Since many junipers bear male and female cones on separate trees, some trees never produce fruits. The seeds of Rocky Mountain juniper are unusual in that they require a 14- to 16-month "after-ripening" period before they will germinate. Changes in moisture and chemical composition occur within the seed during this period, and it can then germinate during the second spring after ripening and falling from the tree.

Seedlings of both species are most successful when they germinate in rocky crevices or other pockets of soil where moisture is trapped. Average height of 8-year-old Rocky Mountain junipers under good growing conditions in the Southwest was only 1 foot. Trees grow slowly, reaching only about 14 inches in diameter in three centuries.

The bark of both these junipers is thin, reddish or gray, and shreds off in strips. Underlying this thin protective layer is a heavy, close-grained aromatic wood. The outer band of sapwood is creamy white, and beneath that is reddish heartwood. The wood of Rocky Mountain juniper is as rose red and fragrant as that of its close relative eastern redcedar (*Juniperus virginiana*), commonly used for cedar chests. In fact, Rocky Mountain juniper is so similar to its eastern kin that Lewis and Clark did not distinguish it as a new species when they encountered it while traveling west into the Rockies in the fall of 1804. The historic common name was "Rocky Mountain red cedar," but this has been replaced in current usage, which is fortunate because it led to confusion with western redcedar (*Thuja plicata*), which also grows in the Rockies.

Because of their generally small size and knotty, twisted trunks neither Rocky Mountain juniper nor western juniper are used regularly for wood products, other than as fence posts and firewood. However, they have been quite important for the latter purposes, especially on the open range where other timber is scarce. Juniper wood is well suited for fencing because it is long-lasting even when in contact with the ground.

Certain groves of Rocky Mountain and western juniper have many trees with almost perfectly spire-like or pyramidal growth forms. Horticulturists have propagated some of these attractive forms through cuttings, and made them available for landscaping.

One other juniper is widespread in the mountain forests of the Northwest, even extending into the alpine zone. However, it rarely grows more than 2 feet high under any conditions in our region. This mat-like shrub is known as common juniper (*Juniperus communis*), appropriately named since it is the only conifer that grows all across both North America and Eurasia. In contrast to Rocky Mountain and western juniper it has small, curved needle-like leaves, arranged in whorls of three on the twigs. Only in the northeastern United States and in Northern Europe does it sometimes develop into a small tree. Common juniper often forms a luxuriant ground cover on stony sites having harsh climates in the West, and it has excellent potential for horticultural use.

Pacific Yew

Taxus brevifolia
Yew family *(Taxaceae)*

Pacific yew is a small tree or large shrub that occupies diverse habitats in our coastal lowlands and mountains as well as the wettest parts of the northern Rocky Mountains — southeastern British Columbia, northern Idaho, and vicinity. Its coastal distribution stretches from the southern tip of the Alaska Panhandle to the San Francisco area. Pacific yew thrives in dense shadows beneath the canopy of western hemlock and Douglas-fir, or at higher elevations, Pacific silver fir. This species not only tolerates shade, in some areas it requires it; consequently when the overstory is logged, yew turns orange and dies back. However, when a new canopy of hemlock, grand fir, and Douglas-fir develops, yew expands in the understory. At middle elevations in some areas of the coastal mountains and in northern Idaho, yew forms nearly impenetrable tangles of sprawling limby growth 10 to 15 feet high, called "yew brush" by foresters.

West of the Cascade Divide, shrubby yews sometimes occupy dry rocky sites and avalanche chutes. Foliage of yews in these exposed sites usually has an orange tinge.

Pacific yew also grows as scattered trees in the coastal lowlands and in mountain canyons, occasionally reaching 2 to 3 feet in diameter and 60 feet in height. I have always found it hard to depict yew as a "little scrubby tree" because as a small boy in the Puget Sound area, the first yew I came to know was a great, limby specimen clothed in 2-inch-thick ivy vines and harboring the neighborhood tree house.

Stout little open-growing yew trees with spreading, limby crowns and weeping branchlets are scattered about in rural areas of the coastal Northwest. They can be identified rather easily by several characteristics: Pacific yew's distinctive foliage

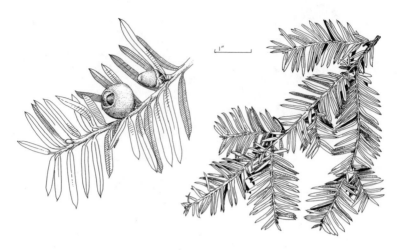

Pacific yew: close-up with fruits and twig

consists of flat, two-ranked needles about ⅔ inch in length, deep
yellow-green on top and pale green underneath. These needles
have slender points at their tips, but they are not sharp to touch.
Moreover, yew needles narrow at the base into a petiole or leaf
stem that extends as a ridge along the twig. New twigs of Pacific
yew are unique among Northwest conifers in remaining green
the year around.

The fruit of Pacific yew is bright red, pea-sized, and resembles
a berry. Technically it is an "aril," since the single seed is sur-
rounded but not completely covered by the fleshy pulp. Yew, like
juniper, bears male and female flowers on separate trees. Also
like junipers, its fleshy fruit is attractive to birds. Consequently,
yew seeds are often distributed across the countryside after passing unharmed through a bird's digestive tract. Yew fruits are
seldom abundant, but their red color insures that birds will
notice them.

Like coastal redwood *(Sequoia sempervirens)* and unlike most
other conifers, Pacific yew can grow permanent sprouts from cut
stumps. Yew can also be propagated from cuttings, and spreads
vegetatively through the layering of lower branches. Coinci-
dentally, yew foliage strongly resembles that of coastal redwood
(which extends north to the southwestern corner of Oregon);
however redwood needles are whitish underneath, and yew
needles are pale green.

While this small, limby tree's form is distinctive, its bark is even more so. Yew bark is very thin, purple, and flakes off in long wavy scales. The wood underneath is almost legendary: the sapwood layer is thin and light yellow, giving way to bright orange or rose-red heartwood; the color alone makes it valuable for small cabinets and decorative works, but more significantly, it is very fine-grained, heavy, hard, very strong but elastic (not stiff), very durable, and responds well to finishing.

Northwest Indians used yew wood for harpoons, bows, and canoe paddles, and wedges for splitting logs. Their yew clubs served in battle and for killing sea lions, and they fashioned this remarkably tough, durable wood into eating utensils.

Historically, English archers, including Robin Hood, used bows made from the closely related English yew, *Taxus baccata,* which is widely planted as an ornamental in Northwest gardens. (English yew can be told from Pacific yew by its more luxuriant foliage.) Pacific yew had drawbacks for archery, since it tends to warp or fracture across the grain and sometimes breaks under strain. However these faults are overcome when bows are made from alternating laminations of Pacific yew and hard maple. These bows are claimed to be best when constructed from yew wood that has dried and seasoned for a few decades. Understandably such bows are an expensive specialty item.

Pacific yew is said to yield excellent canoe paddles because of its strength, hardness, and beauty. However, because of the scarcity of sizeable trees, the species is not harvested commercially. It is a slow-growing tree, reaching at least a few centuries of age, but its age limits are unknown. English yews have been reported to attain ages of between 1000 and 2000 years.

Pacific yew often forms a vigorous, spreading tree when cultivated in the coastal Northwest, whereas English yew usually forms a very large shrub. Pacific yew is the only common tree-like yew in North America; however a low shrub known as Canada yew *(Taxus canadensis)* or "ground hemlock" grows in the northeastern United States and eastern Canada.

Willows

Salix spp.
Willow family *(Salicaceae)*

Willow *(Salix)* is one of the most cosmopolitan genera of trees and shrubs. About 300 species of willows grow in both hemispheres, from the Arctic tundra to South Africa and southern Chile. Over 30 species are native to our Pacific Northwest, but only 8 of these commonly attain tree size. Even these willows are mostly shrub-like trees, with several 20- to 30-foot-tall trunks arising from a single clump.

Willows inhabit every area of the Pacific Northwest, although in the deserts east of the Cascades they are confined to stream courses that run at least intermittently. West of the Cascades and throughout the mountainous areas of the Northwest, willows can be found almost everywhere, but are still most abundant on swampy ground and near water courses. Three species even grow in the alpine tundra, above timberline, where they form extensive lawn-like mats. The branching systems of these dwarf willows lie buried beneath the surface; in August their leaves and catkins thrust up two inches from the frigid ground.

Regardless of size, willows as a group share a distinctive combination of growth characteristics. Their leaves are simple and narrow, or at least longer than broad. A pair of ear-shaped growths called stipules can often be seen at the base of the leaves on new shoots. These stipules are so prominent on vigorous annual shoots such as those arising from a cut stump, that they might be mistaken for leaves. Willows can easily be distinguished from other Northwest trees even in winter by their leaf buds, which are covered with a single cap-like scale. Willow leaves (and buds) are arranged alternately on the twigs.

Despite being deciduous, willows add considerable color to the

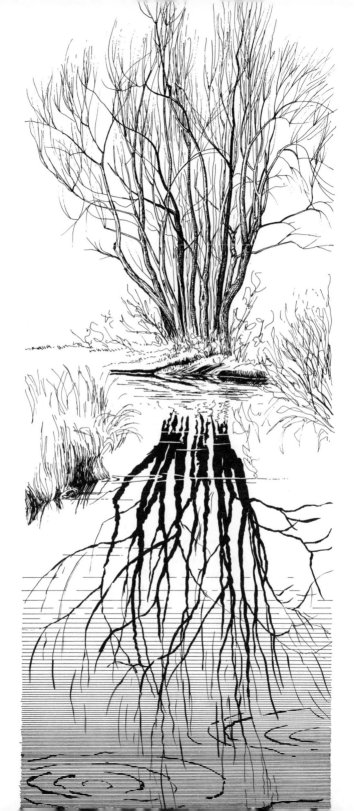

winter landscape, especially where they form dense groves along small streams in semi-arid country east of the Cascades. Depending on the species, these willow patches consist of masses of bright yellow, orange, or red twigs. The annual shoots are tough and withy, as any country kid who has felt the sting of a willow switch can attest!

Late in winter, willow twigs bring the first promise of spring, when the felty catkins known as "pussy willows" appear in advance of the leaves. The female catkins are long narrow clusters of downy flowers that are prized for bouquets. Their male counterparts are often mistakenly collected, since they have a similar felt-like texture; however they should be avoided for bouquets since they shed yellow stamens and pollen about the house.

As spring progresses, the minute individual flowers which make up the female catkin mature into capsules containing seeds so tiny that it takes 2 to 12 million to make a pound. Each seed has a tuft of cottony down which allows it to float long distances in the wind. Willow seeds are also transported to new growing sites by stream water. These seeds are so tiny that they have little stored food or protective covering. Unlike the heavier seeds of most conifers or oaks, willow seeds do not remain dormant over the winter; instead they germinate within about 24 hours of being shed.

Willows usually do not germinate in dry or shady sites and the chances for successful regeneration from the frail seeds are poor. Nature compensates by producing prodigious quantities of seed so that some do happen to land on a suitably moist, sandy site and, under just the right temperatures, regeneration succeeds. Moreover, willow can survive even without seed production since new trees sprout readily from roots and stumps. The trees themselves are composed of light wood that becomes brittle with age; a single trunk seldom survives 50 years.

While the early blooming willow flowers are enjoyed by humans, they are considerably more important to honeybees, providing their first spring food supply. Bees gather pollen and nectar from the catkins for rearing their broods. In fact, willows are immensely important to wildlife in general. They stabilize and shade streambanks, helping keep the water clear and cool, thus maintaining ideal habitat for trout and other aquatic life. Beavers use willow extensively for food, and a great variety of song birds nest in the willow thickets. White-tailed deer, grouse, and any number of other creatures find valuable seclusion in the dense willow groves and deer, elk, and especially moose eagerly chew the younger willow twigs, especially in winter when other nutritious forage is scarce.

Because of their small size and crooked form, western willows are not used for timber, but they do provide good firewood, especially in the semi-arid interior. The tough, flexible shoots are sometimes woven into baskets and furniture. Children find willow useful for willow whistles, slingshot forks, and hot-dog roasting sticks.

Northwest Indians had many uses for willow. They boiled the bitter-tasting bark and used the broth as a remedy for sore throats and tuberculosis. From the bark they also made a twine that was tough enough to serve as the harpoon line for sea-lion hunting. They used willow wood for starting fires by friction, and willow shoots as fish-weir poles, because they take root wherever planted in a stream. (The willow's ability to grow from cut stumps or pieces of branch or root makes it valuable in streamside plantings for erosion control.)

Although it is easy to distinguish willows from other trees and shrubs, identifying individual species of willow can be challenging even to an experienced botanist. In some cases positive identification requires detailed examination of both female and male flowers (catkins), which grow on different plants. To complicate matters, size and shape of the leaves vary substantially within a given species, and if that were not enough, willows often hybridize, producing plants with intermediate characteristics.

Still, it is sometimes possible to identify the more distinctive species without difficulty, and the interested reader should consult volume 2 of *Vascular Plants of the Pacific Northwest* or the condensed *Flora of the Pacific Northwest* (both published by the University of Washington Press). Northwest tree-like willows include the following:

Peachleaf willow *(Salix amygdaloides)* is unique among our tree willows since it occurs only in the semi-arid parts of the Northwest, extending from southeastern British Columbia to eastern Oregon, although it ranges eastward to the Atlantic Ocean. It is especially common along the Snake and Yakima Rivers. It borders streams in rocky or gravelly soil and is the only large willow east of the Cascades, reaching a maximum of 60 to 80 feet in height. The distinctive shiny leaves are long, narrow, and pointed like a peach leaf. This is a picturesque tree with two to four leaning trunks and long, slender, weeping branchlets.

The river or sandbar willows *(Salix exigua, S. fluviatilis,* and *S. sessilifolia)* are three similar species that commonly hybridize. They are found lining streams or ponds at low elevations, and often colonize newly dredged or filled-in sites, spreading by sprouts from their extensive root systems. They are shrubs or very small trees with small narrow leaves that are light green in color.

Hooker willow *(Salix hookeriana)* is a Northwest coast dweller that seldom grows more than five miles from salt water, and even then is restricted to the low-lying streams and marshes. It is often found on coastal sand dunes. Its leaves are distinctively broad and rounded, like English laurel leaves in shape. They have woolly hairs underneath and the younger twigs are woolly also. Its large downy female catkins are the pussy willows par excellence.

Pacific willow *(Salix lasiandra)* grows at lower elevations throughout much of western North America. It is especially abundant in and west of the Cascades, where it characteristically inhabits waterways in a mixture with black cottonwood and red alder. It is very common for instance, in the Willamette Valley, where the larger trees become ragged black-barked specimens 40 to 60 feet in height. Pacific willow foliage can be identified by the two or more wart-like glands found at the base of each leaf blade. Its leaves are distinctively long, narrow, and shiny dark-green.

Scouler or mountain willow *(Salix scouleriana)* inhabits much of western North America, being restricted southward to the higher mountains. It is especially widespread in the Northwest, where it abounds from sea level to an elevation of 7000 feet on the inland mountains. It contrasts from other tree willows in being able to flourish on slopes away from water courses. West of the Cascades it often reaches 30 to 40 feet in height, but on inland or mountain sites it usually forms a tall shrub with many slender, erect stems arising from a clump. This species has also been called fire willow because throughout much of its vast range from the Rockies to Alaska, it readily sprouts or seeds-over large areas which have been swept by forest fires. In northern Idaho and southeastern

Scouler willow

British Columbia, Scouler willow is important forage in the mountain brushfields that serve as prime winter-range for deer, elk, and moose. Some of these older brushfields are being burned by land managers to allow the decadent willows, serviceberry, Douglas maple, and other shrubs to resprout, thereby rejuvenating the forage resource.

Sitka willow *(Salix sitchensis)* is a tall shrub or small tree that grows along streams and other wet sites at lower elevations throughout the moister parts of the Northwest. It is especially common in the lower Columbia River Valley. It has also been called silky willow because of the whitish velvety hairs found on the lower surface of its leaves and on its newer twigs.

Black Cottonwood

Populus trichocarpa
Willow family *(Salicaceae)*

Black cottonwood is one of the tallest and most massive broad-leaved trees in North America, easily surpassing all other broad-leaves in the Northwest. In the rich bottomland soils west of the Cascades the spreading crowns of black cottonwoods reach as high as 175 feet into the cool, moist atmosphere. Such trees may live 200 years or more. These bottomland giants have long branch-free trunks 4 to 5 feet in diameter and covered with thick, deeply furrowed, ashy-gray bark.

Black cottonwood grows along the Pacific Slope from south-central Alaska to southern California, but reaches optimum development and greatest abundance in the Pacific Northwest, where it extends inland along the rivers to Alberta and Montana. East of the Cascades and up in the mountains it does not attain such massive size, but is still the largest broadleaved tree. It inhabits coastal areas receiving 140 inches or more annual precipitation; by contrast, it also occupies deserts east of the Cascades that average only 6 to 8 inches of rainfall annually, although in arid regions, it is confined to streamsides, springs, and lakeshores.

The fact that black cottonwood uses and stores large quantities of water becomes obvious to any woodcutter who fells one of these trees. Even during a dry spell a live cottonwood "bleeds" water; in fact water gurgles and gushes out from the cut stump, and the trunk is so thoroughly saturated that it will scarcely float. However, when the wood dries out it is light in weight.

Black cottonwood can be distinguished from other Northwest trees by its large, broad, almost triangular, pointed leaves. These are deep green above and silvery white on the underside; a gusty summer wind gives the great trees a two-toned appearance. Black

Black cottonwood

cottonwood can also be identified by its large (¾-inch-long) pointed buds filled with a sticky reddish substance that has a sweet resinous smell, and looks and feels like a mixture of honey and strawberry jam.

Cottonwoods, like willows, bear male and female flowers on separate trees. The female flowers mature into 4-inch-long grape-like bunches of light green capsules. The capsules split open in summer, releasing minute plume-laden seeds into the breeze. The cottony-covered capsules and seeds drift through the air day after day and pile up in drifts a few inches deep, so it is obvious to even a casual observer why these trees are called "cottonwood." Black cottonwood germinates best in moist areas which receive full sunlight, and seedlings often cover damp road-cuts or abandoned road-beds.

Black cottonwood is similar in form and features to the balsam poplar *(Populus balsamifera)* of eastern and far-northern North America, and like this eastern kin, it is important for wildlife. Its heavy crown provides splendid sites for the huge platform-like stick nests of bald eagles and ospreys. Canada geese sometimes use these nests, too, and provide quite a sight for bird watchers when they make their landing in the tree top. Colonies of blue herons also build their big stick-pile nests high up in the cottonwoods. Rotten trunks of these large trees are perhaps even more important as wildlife habitat, especially east of the Cascades where other large rotten trees may be scarce. Woodpeckers, great horned owls, wood ducks, flying squirrels, raccoons, and a variety of song birds nest in the trunk cavities. Beavers use cottonwood for food and for building purposes, sometimes chiseling through and toppling trees 2 feet thick — though more often giving up after having chewed only part way through a big tree.

Black cottonwood chewed by beaver

Black cottonwood grows rapidly. In fact, in the lowlands west of the Cascades its growth rate might be best described as phenomenal. Near Camas, Washington, free-growing 9-year-old saplings were found to be 7 inches thick and nearly 50 feet tall. In the Fraser River Valley of southwestern British Columbia, black cottonwoods 27 years old had attained a maximum of 32 inches in diameter and 120 feet in height. The largest-known black cottonwood grows in the fertile Willamette Valley near Salem, Oregon, and is 9½ feet thick and 147 feet tall.

However, this rapid growth does not produce a durable tree. The wood is weak and decays readily in contact with the ground. The large upper limbs split off in strong winds or in snow storms that occasionally come in spring or fall while the leaves are still on, clinging ice often snaps the trees, and the waterlogged trunks may split when they freeze. Black cottonwood is also very sensitive to fire and drought. These characteristics provide ample reason for not constructing buildings beneath a cottonwood, but more important from that standpoint is the fact that black cottonwood is an indicator of soils that are likely to be saturated with water, and perhaps flooded, during part of the year.

As one might suspect, considering its growing site, black cottonwood develops a shallow, spreading root system. New trees can sprout from the surface roots or from cut stumps, and freshly cut twigs will grow into trees if planted in wet ground. Black cottonwood logs left through a rainy winter and spring on railroad cars at Shelton, Washington, were soon covered with a forest of new sprouts.

Black cottonwood is most colorful in autumn when its foliage turns golden; pure stands lining the rivers east of the mountains are especially beautiful at that time of year. Autumn also brings a mounting interest in harvesting black cottonwood for the woodpile. However, the green wood is so wet that it should be split and dried under cover for several months before use. Large rounds of cottonwood may be mushy enough to absorb two steel wedges without splitting, but this resistance can be overcome, especially east of the mountains, by waiting for cold weather, about 10 degrees F. (−12 C.) or colder. The same pieces split easily with a clinking sound when they are frozen.

As firewood, black cottonwood gives off little heat, but it seems to help drive soot out of the chimney when temporarily substituted for the hotter burning (and pitchy) Douglas-fir or ponderosa pine. Although the wood is soft, the outer bark of mature cottonwoods is so hard that it frequently causes sparks when touched with a chain saw. In addition to firewood, black cottonwood is used for making boxes and crates, and when pulped it produces a high grade paper for books and magazines. Northwest cattle also have a special use for this great spreading tree; on a hot summer day 10 to 20 cows will often rest in the shade of a black cottonwood standing in the pasture.

Quaking Aspen

Populus tremuloides
Willow family *(Salicaceae)*

Quaking aspen is perhaps the most colorful tree in the Mountain West. Its leaves, bright green above and silvery beneath, shimmer and whisper almost incessantly in the slightest breeze. Small pure groves of aspen are found tucked away in mountain valleys east of the Cascade Crest, where the prevalent sunshine reflects off their creamy white bark. These groves turn yellow, golden, and occasionally even reddish in fall, beautifying the mountain landscape.

Aspen is especially abundant and well known in the mountains of Colorado, but one need not travel that far to discover this distinctive broadleaved tree. In fact, quaking aspen has one of the widest distributions of any tree in North America. It is one of the few trees ranging from the Atlantic to the Pacific Coast, and its close relative *Populus tremula* inhabits Europe and Asia.

Quaking aspen is an important member of the boreal forest of interior Alaska, Canada, and the northeastern United States, and it extends southward to Virginia and at increasing elevations through the western mountains well into Mexico. However, its affinity for the interior boreal forest zone is evidenced by its scarcity west of the Cascades and Canadian Coast Ranges. Small groves can be found along the lower Fraser River Valley, near Victoria, in the upper Skagit Valley and near Shelton in Washington, and in the Willamette Valley.

By contrast, aspen is widespread east of the mountains. It typically occurs near watercourses, meadows, along canyons (especially in rockpiles) or elsewhere at the edge of the coniferous forest. Although some of these sites may appear to be rather dry, aspen groves generally indicate that water is plentiful

Ramona
Hammerly

just a few feet below the surface at least in spring and early summer. Aspen often becomes abundant on sites where the forest has recently been burned.

Quaking aspen is easy to identify by its sound. Some Indian tribes had names that translate to "noisy leaf" in recognition of its fluttering foliage. The leaves quiver because they are borne on long stalks (petioles) which are flattened or "lopsided" in cross-section. (A person who wants to confirm that the leaf stalk is flattened should try to roll it between his fingers.) Early French-Canadian trappers reportedly believed that this tree supplied wood for the true Cross and since then has never ceased trembling.

Aspen also has other distinctive characteristics. Its smooth cream-colored bark (pale-green on juvenile stems) differs from all other Northwest species. Exceptionally old aspens develop a heavily fissured gray bark on the lower trunk. Unlike its relative, black cottonwood, aspen has small (¼ inch long) shiny dark-brown buds that are not filled with sticky resinous material. But aspen's leaves are even more diagnostic; the blades (1 to 2 inches across) are almost round except for their short, sharp point.

Aspen seeds are tiny (3 million per pound) and are similar to cottonwood in being covered with cottony down. Because they lack stored food or a thick protective coating, the seeds remain viable for only a week or two, and new aspens produced from seeds are considered rarities in some parts of the Mountain West.

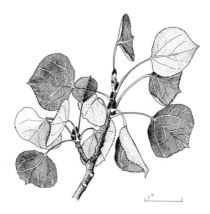

Quaking aspen

Anyone who has tried to yank out an aspen sapling while clearing land soon learns the secret of its regeneration. Usually the sapling is securely anchored to a large horizontal root just a few inches beneath the surface; thus most "saplings" are really just "root suckers." Moreover, most aspen groves are actually "clones," each tree arising from a common root system that has expanded through root sprouting to occupy a sizeable area. Researchers have recently discovered individual aspen clones in Utah that occupy more than 100 acres. Although an individual aspen trunk rarely lives more than 100 years, upon its death it is replaced by new sprouts from the same parent root system. Thus, a clone can probably regenerate for centuries, perhaps even for millenniums, if conditions remain favorable.

Evidence that a single grove of aspens is a genetically identical clone can be seen on a day in early autumn. At this time some aspen groves are uniformly golden, others are yellowish, and others are still green. Evidently the individual clones begin winter dormancy at different times. Scientists have discovered that the date when aspen and many other trees turn color is not necessarily related to the first hard frost, as was formerly believed. Greenhouse experiments varying the length of daylight (photoperiod) have shown that trees of the same species from sites in different latitudes will respond (leaf out, flower, and drop their leaves) to different photoperiods, even when brought to the same site. The activity of each aspen clone may well be a genetically based response to a particular photoperiod.

Since aspen is a short-lived tree that readily regenerates through root suckering or sprouts from cut stumps, it seems reasonable that disturbance would favor perpetuation of this species. Fire or logging does in fact.stimulate aspen regeneration, and equally important, such disturbances hamper invasion by conifers, which are more tolerant of shade and would otherwise replace aspen on many sites.

The larger aspen trunks in a clone often attain 40 to 60 feet in height and 8 to 10 inches in diameter during their modest lifespan. These trees develop a rather distinctive dome-like crown made up of slender, irregularly bent limbs that stand out straight from the trunk. Aspen often grows at higher altitudes in the mountains than other sizeable broadleaved trees and thus it is exposed to and badly broken by clinging wet snow that falls during the period when trees are leafed out — late spring, summer, or early autumn. A foot of heavy wet snow dumped on aspen stands in Glacier National Park, Montana, in June, 1966, caused extensive damage.

Aspen is also injured by animals. It is a choice food for several species of herbivores, and continuous overgrazing, especially by cattle or elk, can eventually cause aspen clones to die — apparently because of incessant drain on their food reserves. Such mortality has been noted in parts of Yellowstone National Park and the Jackson Hole area of northwestern Wyoming where large concentrations of elk feed on apsen.

Ruffed grouse feed extensively on buds and leaves of aspen and spend much of their lives in aspen groves. Snowshoe hares eat the tender bark, as do big game species, often girdling trunks at a point just above the level of the winter snowpack. However, beaver is probably more closely associated with aspen than is any other animal. Beavers spend much of their time logging aspen, cutting it up into chunks, and caching these underwater near their dens for winter snacks. Wildlife biologists estimate that to supply his daily needs, an adult beaver needs to eat the bark off a 2-inch-thick aspen. Aspen bark contains a bitter substance that was used by pioneers as a substitute for quinine, but the acrid taste does not deter beavers or other animals.

Because aspen meant beaver, aspen country was the favorite haunt of early trappers who roamed the Mountain West. The trapper would set an aspen stick strategically in a hole in a beaver's dam to lure the flat-tail to its death in a steel-jawed trap, so that men in Eastern cities could sport beaver hats. By the mid-1800s millions of beavers had been taken and the species was nearly annihilated in many areas; then fashion fortunately changed and beaver, no longer in vogue, gradually made a comeback.

Except for professional photographers who find it a picturesque subject, modern man makes little commercial use of our western aspen groves. In Canada and the northeastern United States, the more extensive aspen stands are harvested for wood pulp to make high-grade paper, and an attractive chip board for walls and ceilings is made by compressing large chips of aspen into paneling.

Aspen is denser than cottonwood and makes good firewood. It

is often propagated by horticulturists, although it should be used with caution as an ornamental since it may develop a spreading root system that could eventually clog sewers or turn the whole yard into an aspen clone!

Alders

(four species) *Alnus* spp.
Birch family *(Betulaceae)*

About 30 species of alder trees and shrubs inhabit moist sites throughout much of the Northern Hemisphere; a few additional species occur southward in the mountains of Central and South America. Like other members of the birch family (but unlike willows and cottonwoods), alders bear both male and female flowers on the same tree. The male flowers appear in showy yellow catkins several inches long; these hang like tassels from the branches in early spring, before the leaves are fully developed. Male catkins are fragile and soon disintegrate.

By contrast, the alder's female fruit is a durable woody catkin (½ to ¾ inch long) that looks superficially like a tiny conifer cone. These hard, dark-brown catkins can be found the year-around on alders, and are diagnostic for identification of alders.

Still another distinguishing feature is the prominent brownish buds that stand out on a short stalk on all but the Sitka alder. Alder leaves are rather large (3 to 6 inches long), egg-shaped, and have sawtoothed edges; they are unusual in being shed in autumn while still essentially green.

Alders are important ecologically (and unique among Northwest trees) because of the way they enhance soil fertility: like legumes, alders have swellings or "nodules" on their roots that convert nitrogen in the air into soil nitrogen. Much of this nitrogen is released to the soil through decomposition of the alder leaf litter.

Although the alders form a distinctive group of trees, and differences between the species of alders are often subtle, it generally is not too difficult to distinguish and identify the four Northwest alders.

RED ALDER — *Alnus rubra*

Red alder is the largest of all alders and the most plentiful and commercially important hardwood tree in the coastal Northwest. It grows at lower elevations in the coastal forests from Yakutat Bay at the north end of the Alaska Panhandle southward to Santa Barbara, California, but it is most vigorous and abundant in the coastal Northwest where it extends from sea level up to about 3000 feet elevation. A few isolated populations have also been found east of the Cascades in moist lowland forests of northeastern Washington and northern Idaho (near Pend Oreille Lake and in protected canyons of the Clearwater River).

Red alder forms extensive stands of trees 10 to 20 inches in diameter intermingled with the second- and third-growth Douglas-fir forests west of the Cascades. These large alders have smooth gray bark that is mottled or sometimes nearly covered with a light-gray lichen. Thus at first glance, they resemble paper birch groves; however paper birch has nearly white bark that shreds off.

Unlike the smaller Sitka alder which is also found west of the Cascades (but at generally higher elevations), red alder has leaves with rounded teeth, and short rusty hairs on their pale undersides. The leaves are normally 4 to 6 inches long, but on vigorous sucker shoots may reach 11 inches.

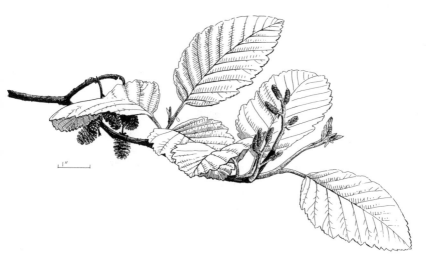

Red alder

Red alder is very intolerant of shade and seldom lives 100 years; nevertheless, it is abundant on moist West Coast sites because it seeds in readily on logged areas and outgrows even Douglas-fir for the first 25 years. Red alder seeds are light (⅔ million per pound) and are showered over virtually the entire west-side landscape by the winds. The trees begin to bear seed at about 10 years of age, and some crops are produced almost every year.

Red alders have a phenomenal early growth-rate, reaching 15 feet in height at 5 years on good sites, 35 to 40 feet at 10 years, and 75 to 80 feet at 25 years. Thereafter, growth slows so that the maximum height of 100 to 110 feet is attained at about 60 years of age. The trees lose vigor rapidly after that time as heart rot sets in. As they die out, more shade-tolerant conifers or even black cottonwoods become dominant. Mature red alders attain diameters of 1½ to 2½ feet.

Historically foresters often regarded red alder as a "weed tree" because it had little commercial value and sometimes prevented reestablishment of Douglas-fir after logging. But, over the past few decades, research has shown that red alder improves forest soils, both physically and chemically. Unlike conifer needles, alder leaves decompose rapidly to form a rich humus, and the root nodules increase soil nitrogen. The result is that Douglas-fir and other conifers grow more rapidly on sites that have been pioneered by red alder.

Prior to the logging era, wildfire and stream-side flooding were the principal agents causing establishment of alder stands in the coastal conifer forest zone. Then, as now, alder groves themselves often served as natural firebreaks since these trees are much less flammable than the conifers. Their foliage and leaf litter does not carry a fire well, and their thin bark is sufficiently resistant to protect them from light surface fires.

Every few years severe outbreaks of tent caterpillars defoliate most of the alders over large areas, but despite the awesome appearance of this damage the trees recover quickly the next year.

Red alder has long been useful to mankind. Some coastal Indian tribes extracted material for a reddish dye from its inner bark; one of the dye's attributes was to make fish nets nearly invisible to fish! Red alder bark steeped in hot water was used by some tribes as a cure for rheumatic fever; interestingly, the bark contains salicin which is a modern medical prescription for this very disease. Coastal Indians also used red alder wood in a variety of woodworkings, including utensils; it was second in importance only to western redcedar for such purposes.

Today red alder continues to supply the coals for that superb Northwest delicacy, smoked salmon. Red alder's good woodworking and staining qualities have made it very useful in making furniture. Alder serves as a clean-burning non-crackling firewood, and it is valuable for horticulture — especially since it often emerges naturally where it is sorely needed to re-vegetate roadcuts and other bulldozed areas or to provide screening in suburban areas.

SITKA ALDER — *Alnus sinuata*

Sitka alder forms dense groves in the snowy mountain forests all across the Northwest. Anyone who has traversed a shrub-filled avalanche swath in the Cascades or our other high mountains will remember the tangles of "slide alder" with its intertwined, spreading stems. These 3- to 6-inch thick, slanted trunks are both tough and springy. Thus, a hiker can hardly walk upon them, but finds it next to impossible to make any headway walking on the ground. Because of their springy stems, these alders often sustain only slight damage in a powerful snow avalanche.

Sitka alder is by any measure a rugged mountain dweller. It is distributed across Alaska, Canada, and coastal Greenland, down the Rocky Mountain Chain through Montana, and along the Cascades and coastal mountains to northern California. It forms a vigorous shrubby growth beyond the limits of conifers in the snowy coastal tundra of southwestern Alaska, and it or a closely related species (the exact relationship is still unresolved) also inhabits the northeastern reaches of Siberia.

From Alaska to Oregon, Sitka alder characteristically pioneers fresh gravelly sites at the foot of retreating glaciers. Studies at such sites in Alaska have shown that this growth of Sitka alder adds nitrogen to the soil at an average of 55 pounds per acre per year, soon fertilizing the glacial ground and preparing it to be reclaimed by the conifer forest.

Sitka alder is probably most easily recognized as the dark-

Sitka alder

green growths covering avalanche swaths on north-facing slopes near all major highways crossing the Cascades and in Glacier National Park, British Columbia as well as in Glacier National Park, Montana. It is widely distributed in moist mountain areas above 3000 feet elevation in the Northwest, usually in the form of a 10- to 15-foot tall shrub. However, it becomes a small tree (about 30 feet tall) where it occasionally extends to lower elevations in mountain canyons and moist places west of the Cascades.

This species is unique among the Northwest alders in that its buds do not have even a short stalk — in botanical terms they are "sessile." Also, its leaves have edges that are "doubly serrate," with sharp little sawteeth superimposed on larger, sharp sawteeth. This is the only alder found in the high elevation forest, where it is abundant there on moist sites as well as on well-drained north-facing slopes. In addition to filling swales where seeps occur and unforested avalanche chutes, it often forms a patchy layer beneath the canopy of subalpine firs, lodgepole pines, or other conifers. Sitka alder's chief values lie in its ability to stabilize snowslides, roadcuts, and other disturbed sites, and to enrich the soil.

THINLEAF ALDER — *Alnus incana*

Thinleaf or mountain alder (also known as *Alnus tenuifolia*) is a large shrub or small multi-stemmed tree (often 6 inches thick and 30 feet tall) that grows along watercourses at lower and sometimes middle elevations within the conifer forests east of the Cascade Divide. Its overall range extends from Fairbanks, Alaska, southward to the inland slope of the Cascades and Sierra Nevada and along the Rocky Mountains into New Mexico and Arizona. It is also closely related to an alder growing in eastern North America and Eurasia; their precise botanical relationships have not yet been determined.

Unlike red and Sitka alders, thinleaf alder seldom grows away from water, and its occurrence indicates the presence of springs, seeps, or streams. It is abundant in these wet sites east of the Cascades. This species can be distinguished from Sitka alder, with which it merges at its upper elevational limits, by the stalk at the base of its buds and the fact that its buds are blunt (versus sharp-pointed in Sitka alder).

Chickadees, pine siskins, and other seed-eating birds of the mountain forests peck away at the little "cones" or female catkins of thinleaf alder to find nourishment in winter and early spring when other food is scarce.

WHITE ALDER — *Alnus rhombifolia*

White alder is a small tree, often with several trunks a foot thick and 50 to 60 feet tall arising from a single clump. It would be most readily confused with red alder except for the fact that, in our area, it occurs mostly east of the Cascades. White alder grows along watercourses in the lower-elevation forests and even in streamside (riparian) stringers extending out into the sage-brush or grasslands. Its distribution extends from southern California through much of Oregon (except for the immediate coast); but from the Columbia Gorge northward, it occurs only east of the Cascades. It grows along the semi-arid lower reaches of the Snake, Clearwater, and Salmon Rivers in southeastern Washington and northern Idaho, and evidently reaches its northern limits on the Okanogan River in north-central Washington.

White alder largely displaces red alder at lower elevations along the rivers in southwestern Oregon, and mingles with red alder in the Willamette Valley. Mature trees can be distinguished by reddish brown, scaly or platy bark on the lower part of the trunk; other alders have smooth gray bark. The leaves have rounded tips (versus distinctly pointed tips in other alders) and lack the rusty tinge found on undersides of red alder leaves. In dry country, white alder is considered to be a more reliable indicator of running water than are cottonwood or willows, because it is usually confined to streams that run all summer.

Paper Birch and Water Birch
Betula papyrifera and *B. occidentalis*
Birch family *(Betulaceae)*

About 40 species of birch trees and shrubs inhabit the Northern Hemisphere, forming a major portion of the forest in the northeastern United States, Canada, Alaska, Siberia, and northern Europe; low shrubby birches occupy vast areas of the Arctic tundra far beyond the limit of trees.

The Northwest has two tree-like birches, paper birch spreading south from the Canadian North Woods, and water birch characteristic of the semi-arid American West. However, these distinctly different species merge and hybridize in the Northwest's interior (in eastern Washington, northeastern Oregon, and northern Idaho) producing a spectrum of intermediate forms. The following characteristics are used to distinguish these species, and to identify intermediate forms:

paper birch	*water birch*
bark peels in sheets	bark does not peel
bark nearly white	bark dark coppery brown
leaf tip with a long sharp point	leaf blunt or only slightly pointed
twigs smooth	twigs covered with warty glands

Paper birch is a major forest tree all across the northeastern United States, Canada, and central Alaska. It inhabits most of British Columbia except Vancouver Island, where it is reported only from the southern tip, and spreads southward west of the Cascades as far as Everett, Washington. It also extends south in moister valleys and canyons of the Inland Empire to northeastern Oregon.

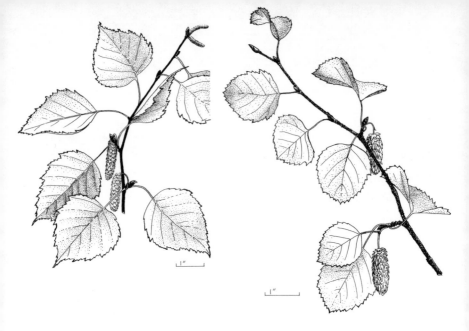

Paper birch   Water birch

West of the Cascades paper birch can be seen along rural roads north of Everett, and especially in the lower Fraser River Valley. Being intolerant of shade, these trees are often seen growing in a pasture or partially cleared area, where they can be identified at quite a distance by their whitish papery bark. Usually two to five trunks arise from a clump or cluster. The largest trees reach 80 to 100 feet in height and 1½ to 2 feet in diameter during their approximately 100-year lifespan.

Paper birch leaves are 1½ to 3 inches long, generally larger than those of water birch, and are rather coarsely toothed. Like alders, all birches bear both sexes of flowers on the same tree. However, the female catkins of birch stand erect and solitary, while those of alder hang in clusters. Also, birch catkins (cylindrical and about 1½ inches long) disintegrate when ripe, unlike the persistent alder "cones." The birch's male catkins start to grow in summer, and sit upright on the twigs all winter; they enlarge and unfold, then hang limp when they mature the following spring.

Birches bear a very small nut (1½ million per pound in paper birch) with a papery wing on each side. These are sometimes produced in prodigious quantities and are spread far and wide by the winds. However, the tiny seeds grow into delicate seedlings that can survive only under a rather narrow range of moisture, light, and seedbed conditions.

Paper birch ▸

Paper birch seedlings grow well on mineral soil or a moist, rotten stump, but on leaf litter they become smothered and unable to grow. Succesful seedlings attain only 3 to 4 inches in height during their first year; by contrast, sprouts from cut or burned stumps grow as much as 2 feet during that time.

If more than a century passes without disturbance such as logging, fire, or a massive blow down, paper birch will be overtopped and crowded out by the longer-lived and more shade-tolerant conifers or even by black cottonwood. Through the ages, wildfire has served as both the killer and the perpetuator of paper birch. These trees are easily killed by fire because of their thin, flammable bark, but fire provides light and growing room for the birch's stump-sprouts as well as mineral soil for its seedlings.

Paper birch bark was used as a fire-starter by North Woods Indians, but it is renowned for its use in birchbark canoes, such as the one made by Henry Wadsworth Longfellow's *Hiawatha*. The bark was peeled in sheets and sewn together over a cedar frame to make a fast, lightweight craft for use on the northern lakes and rivers. The thread was often made from tree roots, and thread holes were filled with balsam pitch. Indians south of Hudson Bay continued to use birchbark canoes at least until the 1950s. Paper birch was also used to make baskets and utensils.

Peeling bark from living paper birch trees is not acceptable in most areas today, however, since it leaves a permanent, unsightly scar by exposing the dark underbark, and it may injure the tree. Useful bark strips can, nevertheless, be taken from a downed tree, since the bark is very durable. In fact the wood in downed trunks of paper and water birch trees often rots away leaving an intact cylinder of birch bark lying on the forest floor.

Paper birch wood is moderately heavy, hard, and strong. It is used for furniture and pulpwood in Canada and the northeastern United States, but has little commercial value in the Northwest, because of its limited quantity here. However, people who live near some of our more extensive stands prize it for firewood, since it splits easily, burns clean, and has a high heating factor. Paper birch and the closely related European white birch *(Betula verrucosa)* also grace most residential areas all over the Northwest. Some of the popular horticultural varieties have weeping boughs, and all can be started from cuttings.

Water birch is a distinctively different but equally interesting tree. Its scientific name means "western birch," which is appropriate since it grows from central Alaska, the Yukon and Manitoba southward to the mountains of Arizona and New Mexico. It

Water birch

grows only east of the British Columbia coast ranges and the Cascades, and its common name is accurate since it is found almost exclusively bordering streams, springs, or other watercourses. This water dependent tree even lines streams in high mountain ranges that drain down into some of the driest deserts, including Death Valley.

Water birch grows along streams at or below the lower

(drought-caused) timberline in eastern Oregon, eastern Washington, southern Idaho, and south-central British Columbia. In these areas it stands out against a backdrop of sagebrush as clumps of spindly dark-stemmed trees averaging perhaps 20 feet in height. This tree looks delicate because of its slender stems and dropping twigs that support a scant foliage of small (¾ to 1¾ inch long), quivering leaves; but this appearance is deceptive, since water birch endures some of the harshest climates in the Mountain West in the high semi-arid valleys of central Idaho, southwestern Montana, and western Wyoming. Hard frosts commonly occur on some of these sites even in midsummer.

In moister mountain areas of the inland Northwest, water birch sometimes reaches 45 to 50 feet in height and 10 inches in diameter. This larger size is particularly common where the trees are apparently hybridizing with paper birch. Even the larger water birches retain the coppery brown bark that does not peel, and their fine twigs are covered with wart-like glands. Often this tree grows squeezed into a slit-like rock gorge where a snow-fed stream gushes over its roots.

Bog birch *(Betula glandulosa)* is the Northwest's only low shrubby birch. It differs from our tree birches in having small, round, leathery leaves, the size of a 25-cent piece. It grows on boggy or marshy sites, sometimes extending up to timberline.

Golden Chinkapin

Castanopsis chrysophylla
Beech family *(Fagaceae)*

Golden chinkapin is an evergreen broadleaved tree seldom seen by people living north of the Columbia River, but relatively common south of the Columbia, in Oregon. Chinkapins *(Castanopsis)* are closely related to chestnuts *(Castanea)* and their scientific name means "chestnut-like." The chinkapins comprise about 30 species of evergreen trees and shrubs worldwide, most of them growing in eastern Asia. Golden chinkapin, the Northwest's only representative, takes on many growth forms, ranging from a lofty timber-producing tree to a sprawling shrub in the forest understory; in this area it most often develops into a small tree 20 to 40 feet tall.

The Columbia Gorge marks the general northern limit of this species, with one stand occurring on the Washington side of the river at Moffett Hot Springs near Bonneville Dam. However, isolated groves of golden chinkapin also grow 130 air-miles farther north near Union on Hood Canal. Golden chinkapin becomes increasingly common on the lower slopes of the Cascades from Mount Hood southward; from Corvallis southward, it spreads to the coast ranges and virtually all of western Oregon.

Open-grown chinkapins develop a dense pyramidal crown composed of deep green foliage which in summer is covered with creamy white blossoms. Since they are tolerant of shade, chinkapins also grow beneath the canopy of Douglas-fir forests; however in these situations their foliage is scant and they often assume a spreading, shrub-like form. By contrast, in the valleys of southwestern Oregon and northwestern California, golden chinkapin sometimes becomes a large tree (maximum 5 feet thick and 127 feet tall), locally known as "giant chinkapin." These trees have straight, clear trunks covered with heavily furrowed bark that is reddish brown on the surface and brilliant red beneath. Still farther south, in central and southern California, this golden chinkapin tree gives way to a shrubby variety of the same species *(C. chrysophylla* var. *minor)* which forms dense patches on warm, dry exposures high in the mountains.

Regardless of its form, golden chinkapin is easily identified by its narrow, leathery, evergreen leaves (2 to 4 inches long, dark green above and yellowish or golden and hairy underneath) and even more distinctive fruit (chestnut-like burs covered with branched or forked spines, which dry to a brownish color in autumn and can be found on the ground beneath most vigorous chinkapin trees or shrubs). Although the burs are abundant, those bearing fertile seeds are often hard to find. The nuts are about ½ inch long and are similar in appearance and taste to our

Golden chinkapin

native hazelnut or filbert *(Corylus cornuta)*. Golden chinkapin can regenerate either from seed or from stump sprouts following fire or cutting.

The male flowers form masses of white spikes (2 to 3 inches long) similar to those of chestnut, and they do an effective job of attracting bees and other pollinating insects on hot summer days. They also give off a musky odor that seems rather rank to humans.

Despite its close relationship to chestnut, golden chinkapin is resistant to the devastating chestnut blight, and is generally little affected by other diseases or insects. When growing as a large tree, it is estimated to survive as long as 500 years. Golden chinkapin is also related to the oaks (also in the beech family) and, at a distance, is difficult to distinguish from the evergreen tanoak tree *(Lithocarpus densiflorus)* of southwestern Oregon and northern California. However, on closer inspection the golden leaf undersides and spiny burs (instead of acorns) readily differentiate golden chinkapin. Both chinkapin and tanoak grow in the chaparral of that region and persist in the understory of the towering coastal forests, including the redwood forest.

In a region where good hardwood timber is scarce, golden chinkapin has been quite useful, especially in earlier times when transportation was poor. Chinkapin wood has a light brown color tinged with pink. It is moderately heavy, hard, and strong, and has been used in agricultural implements and for other purposes where strong hardwood is required.

Oregon White Oak

Quercus garryana
Beech family *(Fagaceae)*

Stout, craggy hardwood trees with dark green foliage and long, crooked limbs grow scattered across a rolling landscape of sunbleached grass. Although these oaks and their setting might be reminiscent of California's golden foothills, they are Oregon white oaks and this scene occurs in the driest areas west of the Cascades from Oregon to southern British Columbia.

Oaks *(Quercus)* are among the most abundant and widespread trees in the world, with perhaps 300 species growing in the north temperate zone as well as in the tropical highlands. About 50 tree oaks are native to North America, and 10 of these inhabit California; however our tree-rich Northwest (North of Eugene, Oregon) has only one oak species.

Botanist David Douglas discovered our Northwest oak in the 1820s and named it for Nicholas Garry, of the Hudson Bay Company, who aided him in his explorations. To this day many Northwesterners know this tree as Garry oak. However, "Oregon white oak" is accepted by the U.S. Forest Service. This name is especially appropriate as seen from a broader, North American perspective, since the tree is most abundant in Oregon, and it is one of the white oaks as opposed to the red or black oaks. The latter's acorns mature in their second year and bear bitter seed, whereas white oak acorns mature in one season and bear sweet seed.

Oregon white oak grows along the southeastern coast of Vancouver Island from Victoria to Nanaimo and northward as far as Courtenay. It occurs in two scattered localities on the British Columbia mainland — Sumas Mountain and Yale, in the Fraser River Canyon. Southward, oak occupies many dry rocky sites in the San Juan Islands and is found at Sequim in the rain shadow of the Olympic Mountains. It grows at scattered localities throughout the Puget Sound Trough, such as in the "Oak Patch" area of Kitsap and Mason Counties and in the dry open woodlands along Interstate 5 south of Tacoma.

Oregon white oak penetrates the Cascades through the rocky Columbia Gorge, and forms scrubby trees northward along the east slope to central Washington's semi-arid Yakima Valley. However, this oak reaches its finest development in the Willamette Valley and Douglas County, Oregon, where its volume exceeds a billion board feet. Here, as elsewhere, it generally grows in the drier valleys (in the 20- to 40-inch annual rainfall zone) inland from the fog-bound coast. Oregon white oak extends also into northwestern California, but is less abundant there, giving way to California black oak *(Quercus kelloggii)* and other California hardwoods.

Oregon white oak can readily be told from other Northwest trees by a number of characteristics. It has a typical "white oak" leaf averaging about 3 inches wide and 5 inches long with 5 to 7 rounded lobes. (California black oak, found with it in southern Oregon, has leaves with bristle-tipped lobes.) The leaves are dark green above and yellow green beneath; their leathery upper surface and hairy underside helps them retain moisure during summer droughts. (April through September rainfall is a meager 4 to 8 inches where the oak grows.)

The fruit is an inch-long acorn enclosed at its base in a shallow saucer-shaped cup. These oaks bear prolific crops of large nuts (averaging 85 per pound) about every other year, and this oak "mast" serves as a favorite food of such diverse animals as pocket gophers, black-tailed deer, mice, squirrels, band-tailed pigeons, and acorn woodpeckers. During some years virtually the entire crop is devoured.

Open-growing Oregon white oaks can be identified at quite a distance by their distinctive form and dark green foliage. The short, thick trunk supports a spreading crown composed of long, gnarled branches. Large trees on the more fertile valley soils develop trunks 3 to 5 feet thick and 80 to 100 feet tall during their 350- to 500-year lifespan.

These venerable oaks are covered with thick, fissured gray bark, but the underlying wood is of considerably more interest to man. Oregon white oak wood equals or exceeds the eastern

Oregon white oak

red and white oaks in most qualities including hardness. It is fine grained, very heavy, very hard, and very strong. Moreover, contributing to its preeminence when used as firewood, is the welcome fact that it splits easily.

The heartwood is durable in contact with the ground; thus its fence posts endure almost as long as western redcedar, and the oak posts are more than twice as heavy and much stronger. Historically, Oregon white oak supplied much of the hardwood lumber needs of the Northwest, being used for boat and ship building, furniture, agricultural implements, and other hardwood construction. Relatively little Oregon white oak is now used commercially, perhaps because its modest supply is distributed on countless farm woodlots and other diverse ownerships and since Northwest lumber mills are built to handle softwoods (conifers). However, the potential for use of this sturdy oak wood may well be realized in the future.

Throughout much of its long life, Oregon white oak suffers from several fungal diseases and insect enemies, but most noticeable is the leafy mistletoe *Phoradendron flavescens.* Large bushy clusters of this parasitic plant grow in the crowns of oak trees, from Portland southward.

Historically, Oregon white oak was favored by the type of land management employed by Northwest Indians. Several tribes harvested and ate the acorns raw or after roasting and other preparation, and some anthropologists suspect that native peoples planted the oaks in the northern part of their present range. More definite evidence of Indians helping to perpetuate the oaks dates back to observations made in 1826 by David Douglas, who reported that the Indians of what is now western Oregon set fires to herd deer and to entice them into feeding in certain areas — the burned sites with their succulent new forage. This periodic burning maintained the oak "savannas" (grasslands with scattered trees) and open oak woodlands with grassy undergrowth that were described by many early visitors to the Willamette Valley.

Settlement put a halt to this burning practice a century ago, with the result that dense thickets of pole-size oaks, Douglas-fir, and other trees have overgrown the former oak savannas. Oregon white oak is very intolerant of shade; thus continued absence of fire on these sites will allow the more tolerant Douglas-fir to replace it. Periodic burning favors the oak since older trees are moderately resistant to fire damage and new life sprouts readily from stumps and root suckers after fire. Also, oak seedlings have a low survival rate in sod or heavy duff, and are more successful when this material has been burned off.

Some species of oak grow almost exclusively on certain types of soils, but Oregon white oak is more of an opportunist, growing wherever it will not be readily crowded out by vigorous conifers. The conifers are not only more tolerant of shade, but also grow faster. These "facts of life" limit oak to the driest habitats, where conifers do poorly. Thus, oak is most abundant on shallow, rock soils and south-facing slopes, especially in Washington and British Columbia. Although some of the sites are so poor that oak develops a shrubby form, this species reaches large size on rich, well-drained alluvial soils where occasional fire, flood, or other disturbance is required to keep it from being replaced by more tolerant trees.

On dry rocky sites throughout its range, the oak's chief companion is Pacific madrone, while on better valley soils it grows with Douglas-fir, bigleaf maple, and Oregon ash. Ironically, one of the oak's principal undergrowth associates in the Willamette Valley is poison oak *(Rhus diversiloba)* — a relationship that newcomers to the area will find worth remembering.

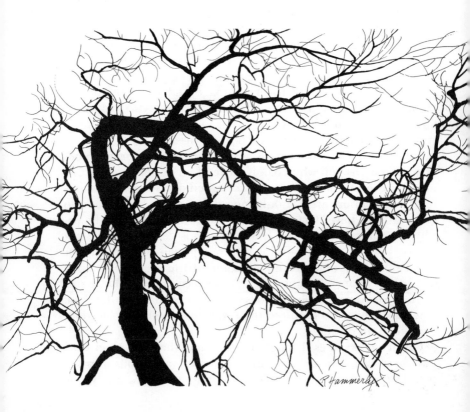

Wild Fruit Trees

Prunus, Pyrus, Crataegus, and *Celtis*

Most of the Northwest's trees that bear edible fleshy fruits are members of the rose family, *Rosaceae,* which includes such valuable trees as the cherry, apricot, peach (all *Prunus* spp.) as well as apple, pear, and mountain-ash. It also includes the blackberries, raspberries, salmonberry, thimbleberry (all *Rubus* spp.), serviceberry, and strawberry.

Two species of wild cherry, a crab-apple, and hawthorn often grow as small trees at lower elevations in our region. The largest of these is bitter cherry, *Prunus emarginata* var. *mollis,* which sometimes reaches 50 feet in height and 10 to 12 inches in diameter west of the Cascade Mountains. Another variety of bitter cherry *(P. emarginata* var. *emarginata)* occurs throughout much of the West, from British Columbia and Montana to the mountains of southern California and New Mexico, generally as a tall shrub.

Both varieties of bitter cherry have oval leaves, 1 to 3 inches long, and not sharp-pointed. They can readily be distinguished from leaves of all other Northwest trees by the pair of knob-like glands attached to the base of most leaf-blades. Small round clusters of fragrant white flowers attract honeybees and other pollinating insects; bitter cherries literally hum with activity in the spring. The flowers mature into round berries (almost ½ inch across) ranging in color from red to black. Despite its bitter taste, the fruit crop is quickly gobbled up by a variety of birds, especially cedar waxwings. The large stone-hard seeds pass unharmed through the birds' digestive systems and are deposited at some other site. Seeds that land in a burned or cutover area or in a moist opening or streamside site have the best chance of becoming established.

Bitter cherry

Bitter cherries west of the Cascades grow rapidly for perhaps 30 years, but then are overtopped and crowded out by red alder, Douglas-fir, and other forest trees. Bitter cherry seldom lives half a century, and its trunk topples and decays rapidly after death. The wood is soft, weak, and brittle, but the tree's distinctive bark, being more durable, is often found as a nearly hollow casing lying on the floor of a second-growth Douglas-fir forest. Mature bark on west-slope bitter cherry trees is dark reddish-brown and has light horizontal bands up to 2 inches long. These bands are actually aggregations of pores called lenticels, which allow air to penetrate to the interior.

Northwest Indians peeled this bark, polished it to a rich red color, and then wove strips of it into their decorative baskets. The east-side variety of bitter cherry is usually a tall shrub; it has smaller, brighter green leaves and gray bark, and often forms dense patches at the edge of streams, meadows, rockpiles, or at the foot of snowslide chutes.

Chokecherry, *Prunus virginiana,* usually develops as a tall shrub, but occasionally forms a tree 30 to 40 feet tall, especially in northeastern Washington. It grows throughout much of North America in several forms and varieties, and is common at

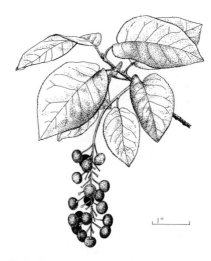

Chokecherry

lower and middle elevations throughout the Northwest, extending out into the semi-arid rangeland east of the Cascades. It has showy, elongated (3 to 5 inches) masses of white blossoms that mature into grape-like clusters of red to black berries. These contrast with the small, short flower and fruit-clusters found on bitter cherry. Also differing from bitter cherry, chokecherry has sharp-pointed leaf tips and has its pair of knob-like glands on the leaf stem (petiole) rather than on the blade.

Choke cherry is an important food plant. In some mountain areas deer and elk eat the foliage and twigs year after year, keeping the shrubs pruned very short. The sour cherries are eaten by birds and bears, and rodents devour the seeds. One naturalist observed that "it takes an Indian to eat chokecherries with a straight face." But Indians and many frontiersmen did eat them raw, and used chokecherries as the major ingredient in pemmican. (To make this, the Indian women pounded cherries, pits and all, on a rock, making a mush to which they added dried meat.) Modern Northwesterners continue to strip these tart little cherries off the shrubs for jelly, jam, chokecherry butter, and wine.

Still another type of cherry found growing wild in Oregon's Willamette Valley is mazzard, *Prunus avium,* a sweet cherry introduced from Europe, which has escaped cultivation and now forms dense shrubby thickets beneath the canopy of second-growth oak forests. Mazzard becomes a good-sized tree when growing in the open, and can be distinguished from the native cherries by its large sweet fruit, large leaves (3 to 6 inches long), and the bark that peels off in strips on mature trunks.

Klamath plum, *Prunus subcordata,* usually grows as a shrub, but sometimes forms a small tree with a stout trunk and broad dome-shaped crown, like a dwarf fruit tree. It can be found at scattered locations in the Willamette Valley, mostly as a shrub, but becomes more abundant and more vigorous east of the Cascades in central and southern Oregon. It can readily be seen growing along pasture fence-lines and stream-sides in the vicinities of Bend and Klamath Lake. It bears a tart but juicy plum, about 1 inch long, that makes an excellent jam. Klamath plum is also distinguished from the cherries by having thorn-like spurs on its twigs.

Klamath plum

Pacific crab-apple, *Pyrus fusca,* is another native fruit tree with thorn-like spurs on its twigs. (These spurs differ from true thorns since they bear buds.) It inhabits the damp foggy coastal forest zone from south-central Alaska to northern California and often borders beach meadows or swamps along the ocean front. It grows at low elevations in and west of the Cascades in moist pasture and streamside thickets with red alder, willows, bigleaf maple, and cascara. Pacific crab-apple leaves are egg-shaped, 2 to 3 inches long, and often have shallow lobes or notches like those of domestic apple trees. Another scientific name for this species, *Pyrus diversifolia,* gives recognition to its diverse leaf shapes. The

Pacific crab-apple

leaves are a dull dark green on the upper surface and generally have whitish hairs underneath. They turn scarlet and bright-orange in the fall.

Pacific crab-apple bears typical apple blossoms. The flowers in these clusters are waxy, and white or rose-colored, with a delightful fragrance. The apples themselves are oval, about ¾ inch long and yellow with pink cheeks, hanging in small clusters from rather long stalks. Their flesh is thin, rather dry, and extremely sour, but makes good home-canned preserves and is also appreciated by grouse, bears, and probably other animals.

Pacific crab-apple has been known to science since it was first described in 1792 by naturalist Archibald Menzies, who found it at Port Discovery, east of present-day Port Angeles, Washington. It often forms scrubby thickets along the coast, but develops a trunk 8 to 10 inches thick and 20 to 30 feet tall under less-exposed conditions. It grows slowly, reaching 100 to 150 years of age, and forming wood that is fine-grained, heavy, and hard. Northwest Indians used Pacific crab-apple wood for the prongs of their seal spears and for wedges to split western red cedar. Early grist mills in Ontario, Canada, used a similar crab-apple wood for their gears.

One of our wild fruit trees has "true" thorns and "false" apples: black hawthorn, *Crataegus douglasii,* grows at lower elevations throughout the Northwest, being especially common along streams, ditches, and in valley bottoms. Although more than 100 species of hawthorn inhabit North America, only two species grow in the Northwest. (The other is *Crataegus columbiana* which occurs in scattered locations east of the Cascades and is distinguished by its 2- to 2½-inch-long thorns.) Black hawthorn has thorns ½ to 1 inch in length. These are slender, sharp, and tough, as anyone who has snagged his clothing on them will attest. The twigs themselves grow in a zig-zag fashion which enhances the density of these little trees. That hawthorns make a good hedge was recognized by medieval Anglo-Saxons whose word "haw" meant hedge.

Black hawthorn leaves are 1 to 2 inches long and often rather fan-shaped, with small shallow lobes or deep notches, but quite variable. The flowers are white and reminiscent of apple blossoms. The black hawthorn itself is generally a multi-stemmed shrub or small tree, attaining 20 to 30 feet in height on rich alluvial soils.

Black hawthorn

"Thorn apple" is another name sometimes applied to hawthorns in recognition of their miniature apple-like fruit. The fruit of black hawthorn is black, about ½ inch long, and contains 3 to 5 bone-hard seeds. Although these small, dry, stony fruits are of little use to man, they are valuable as food for several species of birds, especially since they remain on the tree all winter.

In semi-arid country east of the mountains where both magpies and hawthorns are abundant, nearly every large hawthorn holds at least one magpie nest. Often a single clump will harbor two or three of these intricately woven spiny stick-pile nests, one of which is the birds' current abode. The magpies negotiate their way through this dense thorny foliage with amazing ease and agility.

Many Northwesterners have noticed craggy little fruit-bearing trees growing in the arid, rocky, otherwise treeless gorges of the Columbia, Deschutes, and Snake Rivers, east of the Cascades. Although this species is quite conspicuous, and has several distinctive characteristics, few people learn its identity.

This "strange little tree" is netleaf hackberry *(Celtis reticulata).* Despite the fact that 150 species in this family (including the hackberries and elms, *Ulmus)* are widely distributed throughout temperate regions of the world, this is the only member of the elm family *(Ulmaceae)* native to the Pacific Coast states. Netleaf hackberry is essentially the only tree that extends north into our area from the desert Southwest. It is abundant in northern Mexico and as far north as southern Utah, reaching its northern limits in the arid coulees of north-central Washington (Douglas County). It can be seen along the highway on the south side of the Columbia east of The Dalles, in the Deschutes and John Day river canyons, and along the Snake River in southeastern Washington. It is the only common tree in the bottom of mile-deep Hells Canyon in northeastern Oregon and adjacent Idaho.

Rather than lining the watercourses like cottonwood and willows, hackberry generally occupies rocky sites above the water. It is very tolerant of drought, growing in regions that receive as little as 7 inches of annual precipitation, and where summer temperatures reach 110° F. (43° C.) or more.

Considering these growing conditions, it is not surprising that netleaf hackberry becomes a squatty dwarf, with a crooked trunk only about a foot thick and 20 to 30 feet tall at maturity. Still, it produces an extensive network of twisting limbs that supports dense foliage. The leaves are 2 to 3 inches long and egg-shaped, but like those of elm they are lopsided at the base (one side being larger than the other). They are thick, dull green, and feel rough or coarse. The tree's common and scientific names both denote the prominent network of veins visible on the underside of its leaves.

This thick foliage hides most of the cherry-like fruits, which are ¼ to ⅓ inch thick and are attached singly at the base of each leaf

Netleaf hackberry

near the branch tips. These "hackberries" range in color from yellow to orange and red, and they have a sweet dryish pulp covering a large bony seed. They can be picked (mostly by birds) as late as mid-winter, a season of short duration in the hot east-side canyons where the hackberries grow.

Bigleaf Maple

Acer macrophyllum
Maple family (*Aceraceae*)

Of the 115 species of maples that inhabit the Northern Hemisphere, 13 grow in North America. Three maples are native to the Northwest, but only the beautiful, interesting, and useful bigleaf maple becomes a good-sized tree.

Bigleaf maple occupies the coastal lowlands from just south of the Alaska Panhandle in British Columbia (where it is limited by cold), through the western portions of Washington and Oregon. Farther south in the warmer, drier climate of California, it is restricted to moist canyons at increasing elevations in the coast ranges and Sierra Nevada. It is abundant west of the Cascade Divide from southern British Columbia to southern Oregon from sea level to 3000 feet elevation, and it also reaches its best development here. (It occupies a few of the moister canyons on the east slope of the Cascades.) Mature open-growing trees have short trunks, 3 to 4 feet thick, that support massive, spreading limbs. Such trees are 70 to 80 feet tall and equally broad; they often survive 200 years.

Bigleaf maple is easily distinguished from other native and introduced maples by its giant leaves, 8 to 12 inches across, with five lobes deeply cut into them. The leaf stalks are 6 to 12 inches long and differ from those of other maples in exuding milky sap when broken. All maples bear their leaves, twigs, buds, and winged fruits opposite each other in pairs, which facilitates year-round identification.

In late April and early May the translucent new leaves are unfolding and only half-grown, while copious clusters of fragrant yellow blossoms 4 to 6 inches long hang from the boughs. These nectar and pollen-bearing blossoms teem with honeybees and other insects on warm spring days.

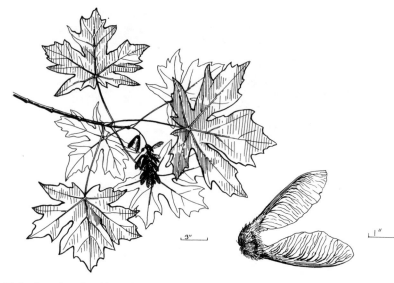

Bigleaf maple twig with seeds; close-up of the fruits

Maples depend on insects for fertilization of their flowers, and evidently these creatures perform admirably, since bigleaf maple is a prolific seed producer. Its fruit, like that of other maples, is known as a double samara and consists of two nuts with long (1½ inch) wings attached in a horseshoe shape. This species begins to bear fruit when only 10 years old, and some of the crop hangs on the trees through fall and winter, providing nutritious food for Douglas squirrels, finches, and evening grosbeaks when pickings are generally scarce.

In spring, countless seeds from the previous season's crop can be found germinating on the forest floor. Seeds of this and other maples also germinate in cracks in the sidewalks in Northwest cities. In the forest perhaps only one in a million of these new seedlings will be able to root into mineral soil in a spot where there is adequate growing space for it to survive and grow into a large tree. Chances for establishment are best in cut-over or other disturbed sites, although this species is tolerant of shade and can regenerate even in the dense coastal forests, where there is an opening beneath the towering conifers.

For example, bigleaf maples are a prominent feature of the Olympic rain forests. In these super-humid environments, large maples are clothed with drapes of hanging moss, which undoubtedly weigh a ton or more when wet. Bright green licorice ferns grow out of the moss litter high up in these venerable trees.

Bigleaf maple blossoms

Bigleaf maple achieves its best growth in rich bottomland soils and is probably the commonest native shade tree in towns and pastures west of the Cascades. One aged maple, 7 feet thick, still stands on the highest point of Sauvie Island in the Columbia River near Portland marking the site of a trading post established more than 150 years ago. A tree more than 8 feet thick and 96 feet tall growing near Salem, Oregon, is the largest of any species of maple in North America.

Although very old trees often have rotten boles, this species is valued for lumber and fuel wood. The heartwood is light reddish-brown, fine-grained, moderately heavy, and moderately hard and strong. It takes a high polish, and often has interesting grain patterns, such as "curly" or "bird's eye maple." It is used principally for making veneer for furniture.

Northwest Indians found both the bigleaf and vine maples

quite useful: they used the bark in making rope and carved the wood into bowls, utensils, and canoe paddles. Modern Northwest children have chosen bigleaf maple as their favorite species in which to build tree houses, and song birds evidently agree, since a large spreading maple generally harbors several nests.

Bigleaf maple is often planted as a shade tree in England, as well as in our area, but it is not successful in climates having cold winters. Still, like some of its eastern kin, it turns a beautiful color (bright orange-yellow) in fall, and, perhaps surprisingly, it can yield maple sugar in nearly as good quality and quantity as eastern sugar maple. Evidently production of this maple sugar is not yet practical commercially (the USDA Forest Service's Pacific Northwest Experiment Station, headquartered at Portland, has published a report on how to produce sugar from bigleaf maple).

Squirrel extracting bigleaf maple seed; close-up of empty shell

Bigleaf maple in rain forest

Vine Maple and Douglas Maple

Acer circinatum and *A. glabrum* var. *douglasii*

Maple family (*Aceraceae*)

Two species of small or shrubby maples inhabit Northwest forests; both are readily recognizable in early autumn when they light up the mountainsides with red and orange, and new shoots of both are a favorite food of deer and elk. However, this is about where the similarities end and the contrasts begin in comparing these two little trees.

Residents west of the Cascades are most familiar with vine maple, the "octopus" of the shady forest where it often sends its long, tough limbs spreading and sprawling about the understory. Like Pacific yew, vine maple grows well in dense shade. Its stems are often flattened to the ground by heavy wet snows, and these prostrate limbs occasionally root into the damp forest duff and soil.

Thus, vine maple is a characteristic understory tree of the moist western hemlock and Douglas-fir forests at lower elevations (mostly below 3000 feet) extending from the Cascades to the Pacific shore. Although abundant in the area (as many an outdoorsman who has traversed some of its domain will attest!), its overall distribution is quite restricted. It grows from southwestern British Columbia to northwestern California, and is not found inland from the Cascades. However, it is apparently absent from Vancouver Island, which is surprising considering the wet forest habitats there.

Vine maple was well known to the Quinault Indians of Washington's Olympic Peninsula, who referred to it as "basket tree" because they wove its long, straight shoots into open baskets used for carrying clams and fish.

In addition to its rather distinctive growth forms and its habitat, vine maple can be readily identified by its foliage: the

Vine maple

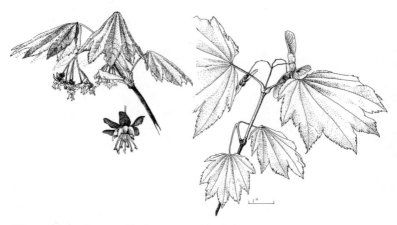

Vine maple in flower (with close-up) and in fruit

leaves average 3 to 4 inches across and are rather star-shaped, with seven to nine sharp-pointed lobes. Some of them begin to turn red or yellow as early as midsummer, and they produce an unforgettable display of colors in October. The fruits turn reddish also, and they differ from those of our other maples in having wings that spread out in opposite directions.

When it grows in clearings and avalanche chutes, or when it is cultivated as an ornamental, vine maple forms a bushy multi-stemmed tree 20 to 30 feet tall; in these instances it resembles the Northwest's other small maple, the Douglas maple, which is well known to residents east of the Cascades. It is widespread in the West, reaching from southern Alaska through the mountains of central California and inland to western Montana. Moreover, another variety of the same species (var. *glabrum*), called Rocky Mountain maple, extends southward through the Rockies at increasing elevations to southern Arizona and New Mexico.

Douglas maple is less common west of the Cascades, but grows at scattered locations in the Puget Sound area and elsewhere especially on dry, open rocky sites including canyon walls and bluffs. Some exceptionally large trees, 12 to 15 inches thick and 40 feet tall, have been found at Birch Bay, north of Bellingham, Washington. Unlike vine maple, it is intolerant of shade, and grows best in open areas, forming a clump of upward pointing branches. It has a small leaf (2 to 5 inches long) with only three or five main points; the new twigs are generally bright red.

In and east of the Cascades, Douglas maple forms a major component of some brushfields (along with Scouler willow, serviceberry, chokecherry, etc.) that serve as prime winter range for mule deer and elk. Often the maple clumps appear to have been pruned, which in fact they are—by the wild herbivores. When an elk herd has dined on maples, these shrubs look as though they had been thrashed with a dull scythe!

Douglas maple with fruits

Cascara Buckthorn

Rhamnus purshiana
Buckthorn family (*Rhamnaceae*)

Although cascara buckthorn is a little tree having no value for timber, it provides an essential ingredient in medications used throughout the world. As much as five million pounds of dried cascara bark from the Pacific Northwest has been processed in a single year by pharmaceutical companies in the manufacture of laxatives.

Cascara grows at lower elevations from northern California to southern British Columbia and is widespread west of the Cascades and British Columbia Coast Range. It also inhabits a few of the moister canyons on the east slope of the Cascades, and occurs in northern Idaho, northeastern Washington, southeastern British Columbia, and northwestern Montana. West of the Cascades, cascara often develops a single trunk 8 to 12 inches thick and 20 to 35 feet tall, although trees this size are scarce in areas where "chittam bark" peelers have been at work. It is very tolerant of shade and thus often occurs in the understory of second growth forests. It is most commonly found with red alder in moist bottomlands, but even then is not abundant.

Although it grows mixed with several other deciduous trees and tall shrubs, cascara has several characteristics that make it easy to identify. Its leaves are oblong and generally 3 to 5 inches in length, but unlike leaves of other Northwest trees, these have 10 to 12 pairs of prominent parallel veins arising directly opposite each other on the midrib. Although they are generally alternate in arrangement on the twigs, leaves on new growth are often attached nearly opposite each other.

Positive identification can be made in winter using the buds, because they are unique among those of Northwest trees in

being naked; that is, cascara buds have no scales to cover the tiny, folded embryonic leaves and shoots. Only a layer of brownish woolly hairs protects the buds.

Cascara flowers are greenish and rather inconspicuous in their small spherical clusters. However, in midsummer they produce a more noticeable fruit, a round blackish berry about ⅓ inch in diameter, which is edible although little used by mankind, but devoured by raccoons, grouse, and a variety of other birds and mammals. Birds void the seeds unchanged, evidently planting many new cascara trees in the process.

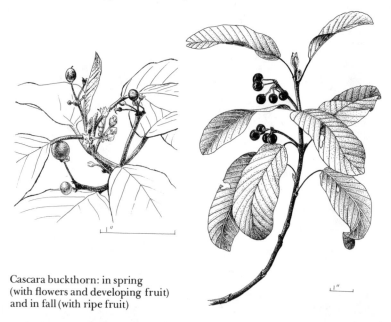

Cascara buckthorn: in spring
(with flowers and developing fruit)
and in fall (with ripe fruit)

When in doubt, a person can always tell cascara by cautiously tasting its bark. When chewed, fresh "chittam bark" is intensely bitter and can temporarily numb the taste buds. Northwest Indians prepared it as a laxative, tonic, and cure-all. (They also produced yellow and green dyes from it.) Occasionally it was administered in an overdose that proved fatal.

The name "cascara sagrada," used in medicinal trade, means "holy bark" in Spanish, and was apparently derived from its use by Franciscan missionaries in California. Cascara bark has been harvested commercially for 100 years, and demand has remained strong despite the development of synthetic laxative agents. The bark is smooth and gray or brownish, often resembling that of young red alder. It is peeled in strips, dried, and aged to make it milder. Peeled trees should be felled so that the stumps and root systems will survive and resprout. Many of the multiple-stemmed cascaras found in rural areas today are in fact sprouts from a previously harvested tree.

The bark from a 6-inch-thick tree is said to produce 2000 doses of "natural" laxative. Cascara bark was in heavy demand during World War II, when it was used in "CC" pills that were often prescribed for ailing servicemen. More recently, some enterprising rural Northwesterners have started small plantations of cascara. Experienced cascara-bark peelers wear gloves; they have discovered that stripping the fresh bark bare-handed has a laxative effect!

Alderleaf buckthorn, *Rhamnus alnifolia*, is a closely related, medium-sized shrub that grows in moist forests east of the Cascades. It can be distinguished from cascara by 5 to 7 pairs of

Ceanothus, with close-up of flower

parallel leaf veins (versus 10 to 12 on cascara). The genus *Ceanothus* makes up another interesting group of shrubs in the same family (*Rhamnaceae*). One of these species, *Ceanothus velutinus* variety *laevigatus*, called mountain balm, greasewood, sticky-laurel, or shiny-leaf ceanothus warrants mention because it sometimes forms a spreading tree 15 to 20 feet tall in the lowlands west of the Cascades. This growth form is particularly confusing since another variety of this species (var. *velutinus*) is abundant east of the Cascades, where it forms a shrub only 2 to 6 feet tall. Wherever it grows, this species is readily identified by its unusual oval evergreen leaves about 3 inches long; they are thick, gummy, glossy dark-green, and have three prominent veins.

Pacific Dogwood

Cornus nuttallii
Dogwood family (*Cornaceae*)

Although Pacific dogwood is the most beautiful flowering tree in Northwest forests, its true "flowers" are small, greenish, and inconspicuous. However, these plain flowers are set in a cluster of creamy white floral leaves (bracts) that create a gleaming blossom 4 to 6 inches across. Dogwoods brighten the understory beneath our towering Douglas-fir forests in late April and May, and bloom even more profusely in open areas and in Northwest cities, where, uncrowded, they develop denser crowns.

Dogwood's color display is not limited to springtime. By September the inconspicuous true flowers have ripened into a cluster of bright red fruits (about 1 inch across) nestled among leaves that range from green to orange, red, and purple. Some trees even flower again at this time of year.

This little tree is especially unusual because it commonly grows and blossoms in the somber shade at the foot of giant conifers—a habitat in which relatively few hardwoods can prosper. In fact, Pacific dogwood is found in all the gigantic West Coast forests, including those dominated by skyscraping Sitka spruce, Douglas-fir, coastal redwood, and giant sequoia. Studies of the closely related eastern dogwood have revealed one secret of its successful growth beneath the conifer canopy: dogwood carries out maximum photosynthesis under only one-third of full sunlight.

Pacific dogwood is confined to lower elevation forests in and west of the Cascades, from southern British Columbia to northern California, and also grows southward at increasing elevations in the mountains of central and southern California. Only one isolated occurrence of this species is known inland from

Pacific dogwood: in spring (with blossom)
and late summer (with fruit)

the Cascades. In May it illuminates the rugged Lochsa River canyon in northern Idaho, along the Lewis and Clark Highway (U.S. 12).

This species forms a slender-trunked, spreading tree usually 30 to 50 feet tall, that lives as long as 150 years. Its leaves, twigs, and buds are borne opposite each other, and the leaves themselves have opposite pairs of prominent veins that curve parallel to the leaf margin. The leaves are oval and 4 to 5 inches long.

The dense spherical cluster or "button" of red, berry-like fruits attracts a variety of birds. Interestingly, the blossoms, fruits, and leaves of this tree are strikingly similar to those of a small herb commonly found growing on the forest floor. This little plant, known as bunchberry dogwood (*Cornus canadensis*), is a member of the same genus. One other dogwood occurs in the Northwest, a tall shrub called red osier dogwood (*C. stolonifera*) that has shiny red twigs and clusters of small white blossoms, and usually grows along streams.

However, the most prominent relative of Pacific dogwood is flowering dogwood (*Cornus florida*), a very similar tree indigenous to the eastern United States. The resemblance between these

Bunchberry dogwood

two trees is so close that David Douglas, the first botanist to see Pacific dogwood, mistook it for the eastern species. In the 1830s, a decade after Douglas's visit, the American naturalist Thomas Nuttall examined the beautiful dogwoods of the Pacific slope and found, among other differences, that our dogwood has four to six floral bracts (vs. four in eastern dogwood) and that its blossoms are larger than those of the eastern species. Nuttall observed that although the red berries are somewhat bitter, they are the favorite autumn food of band-tailed pigeons.

Humans have also had several uses for dogwood: some Northwest Indians boiled the bark to make a laxative, and the tannin-rich bark was used by some frontiersmen in place of quinine to cure malaria. The wood is heavy, hard, and whitish, like that of eastern dogwood, which has been used extensively for shuttles in textile mills, and for golf club heads and piano keys. Landscaping has been the chief use of Pacific dogwood, and horticulturists would be interested to know that a form with pink blossoms has been found on Vancouver Island.

Even the name "dogwood" may relate to an early use of these hardwood trees. Evidently the wood was considered especially suited for skewers or "dags" and in time "dagwood" became "dogwood."

Pacific Madrone

Arbutus menziesii
Heath family (*Ericaceae*)

Pacific madrone could hardly be mistaken for any other Northwest tree. It is the only broadleaved evergreen tree found in any appreciable quantity north of the Columbia River (southward as far as Eugene, Oregon, the only other broadleaved evergreen is the scarcer golden chinkapin, distinguished by its spiny burs). Another distinctive feature of madrone (also called madrona and madroño) is its papery bark, which shreds off in ragged, crinkly strips and ranges in color from greenish or chartreuse on younger stems to reddish on some twigs, orange on young trunks, and darkening on old trunks to brown with flaky gray scales. Madrone's kaleidoscope of color is rounded out by the dark glossy green leaves and, depending on the season, white to pinkish flowers or red to orange fruits.

Madrone inhabits coastal lowlands from the vicinity of Seymour Narrows (50 degrees N.) in southern British Columbia to southern California. It is especially widespread and common in the lowlands west of the Cascades in Washington and Oregon, but southward in California it is confined to scattered sites in the Sierra Nevada as well as along the immediate coast. Early Spanish Californians first called this tree madroño, meaning "strawberry tree," because they recognized its resemblance to the strawberry madrone (*Arbutus unedo*) of their Mediterranean homeland. (Two other madrones grow in North America, in Texas and southern Arizona, where they prosper in hot, dry climates.)

Pacific madrone is restricted to an area having mild oceanic winters; however, it occupies sites where average annual precipitation ranges from 150 down to 15 inches. It grows on many types of soils, but becomes most abundant on rocky sites such as

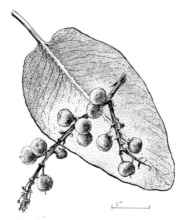

Pacific madrone: leaf and fruit

bluffs overlooking saltwater inlets; madrone is often silhouetted
with its trunk arching out over the salt water and its foliage
nearly lapped by the waves at high tide.

It is moderately tolerant of shade, but most numerous on dry
or stony sites where the conifer forest does not readily close in. It
rarely grows in pure stands, and is associated principally with
Douglas-fir, and in the Willamette Valley with Oregon white oak.
It inhabits the driest sites in the San Juan Islands and on south-
facing hillsides in southwestern Oregon, but is generally
reduced to a small, often scraggly tree or shrub under severe
conditions.

In more favorable situations madrone grows 50 to 80 feet tall
and 2 feet in diameter, usually with a broad, spreading crown
supported by multiple, curved trunks and heavy, irregular
branches. These trees can survive two centuries or longer, and
occasionally attain great size when growing in the open or fertile
valley soil or in a city. The largest known specimen, growing in
northern California, is nearly 10 feet thick with a maximum
crown spread of 126 feet.

As anyone who has one in his yard can attest, madrone is an
active and messy tree. In May it bears clusters of small white to
pinkish bell-shaped flowers that resemble those of many shrub
members of the heath family including kinnikinnick and
manzanita *(Arctostaphylos)*, mountain heath *(Phyllodoce)*, and
huckleberries *(Vaccinium)*. These showy flowers have a strong,
sweet odor that attracts honey bees.

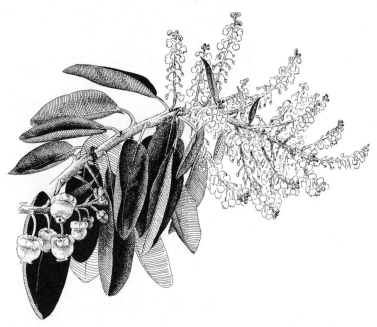

Pacific madrone, with close-up of flower cluster

In June, the second-year leaves turn orange to red and begin to fall, shortly after the new crop of leaves has become fully grown. The leaves are 3 to 6 inches long and about half as wide. They are thick, leathery, and mostly smooth-margined except for those on vigorous young growth which sometimes develop saw-teeth. Living leaves are dark glossy green above and whitish green below, and resemble leaves of evergreen rhododendron, also in the heath family.

Madrone sheds bark all summer, leaving behind a thin, smooth skin. As one might suspect, this provides scant protection from fire; however madrone readily sprouts from the stump after burning.

Clusters of orange-red berry-like fruits ripen in autumn and persist into December. These pea-sized fruits have a roughened, granular surface and a mealy pulp surrounding a knot of small, bony seeds. Madrone fruits are a favorite food for several species of birds including band-tailed pigeons and quail, and they are reported to have narcotic properties. Birds are believed to be a major factor in disseminating, and inadvertently planting, madrone seed.

Good fruit crops are borne regularly, as are bark crops, and leaves; thus madrone sheds leisurely during about half the year, affording homeowners plenty of good exercise through raking! Despite this drawback, madrone is a popular natural ornamental, which can be propagated from cuttings.

Northwest Indians ate madrone berries and made spoons and small dippers from the somewhat bulbous roots. Madrone wood is pale reddish-brown, heavy, dense, and has a fine, twisted grain. It cuts like a softwood when green, but becomes very hard when dry. It makes good firewood and charcoal, and a person who splits it will also generate considerable body heat! Madrone checks badly in normal drying and has had little commercial use, but it has occasionally been made into flooring, and tests have shown that it will produce a handsomely figured veneer.

Oregon Ash

Fraxinus latifolia
Olive family (*Oleaceae*)

Oregon ash might be thought of as a typical eastern hardwood tree that somehow got misplaced and occupies the conifer-dominated Northwest forests. Although there are nearly 500 species of trees and shrubs in the olive family (*Oleaceae*) — including the edible olive, lilacs, forsythias, privets, and ashes — Oregon ash is the only member of the entire family native to the Northwest. Sixteen ashes grow in the United States and four of them are important timber trees in the East and Midwest. Oregon ash reaches a comparable size and has similarly useful wood, but is less abundant than its eastern kin, and has a smaller natural range.

It inhabits nearly all lowland valleys west of the Cascades from the Seattle and Aberdeen areas of Washington south to northern California, being especially abundant in the Willamette Valley. It also occurs in a smaller form along mountain streams in central California. In the Northwest, it commonly occupies moist bottomland sites as well as bordering wet meadows, swamps, and streams. It grows with grand fir, Douglas-fir, and several broad-leaved trees — including bigleaf maple, red alder, and black cottonwood, but it is easily distinguished by its oppositely arranged, compound leaves.

These leaves are mostly 6 to 12 inches long and are composed of five to seven oval leaflets attached in pairs to the leaf stalk with an additional one at the tip. The leaves are lighter in color than those of other trees, and they turn bright yellow before dropping in autumn. They usually have a coating of woolly hairs on their undersides. Winter identification of this species is made easy by the twigs that are oppositely arranged (and bear opposite

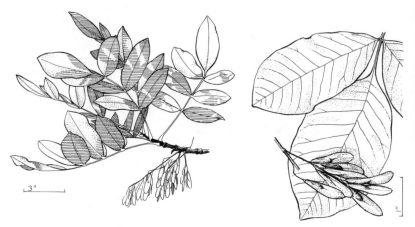

Oregon ash: twig and close-up of leaf and fruits

buds) as well as being stout and covered with woolly hairs. Oregon ash flowers are small and rather inconspicuous, and male and female flowers are borne on separate trees. Thus, only female trees produce the clusters of ash fruits. These are winged "samaras" like those of maple except that ash samaras are single, while maple samaras are fused together in pairs. Oregon ash samaras are 1 to 2 inches long and shaped like the blade of a canoe paddle. Heavy seed crops occur at three- to five-year intervals; this species also regenerates from stump sprouts.

Even the bark of Oregon ash is quite distinctive. It is thick and heavily ridged, and the vertical ridges are joined at a slant by thinner side ridges, creating a woven appearance.

When growing in open areas such as pastures, this species forms a broad, spreading crown rather like bigleaf maple. However, it is intolerant of shade, and in the usual, more crowded conditions its growth is channeled skyward; thus it becomes a tree 60 to 80 feet or taller, with a narrow crown. Despite the moist to wet nature of its habitat, Oregon ash is considered exceptionally windfirm by virtue of its massive, spreading root system. These trees grow rapidly in youth, but then slow down considerably during the latter part of their lifespan, which is often two centuries.

It may seem surprising that the wide-ringed young growth is the most valued wood. Inspection of a good baseball bat, shovel or axe handle will usually reveal wide-ringed ash growth —

probably from an eastern species, although Oregon ash has similar wood. The explanation is that wood from fast-growing ash is elastic, whereas the fine-grained growth of older trees is more brittle. However, this latter characteristic makes older trees ideal for firewood, since they split easily. Incidentally, Oregon ash is second only to Oregon white oak in heating value.

Because its eastern relatives are much more abundant, Oregon ash has had minor commercial use, but ash in general is a standard material for tool handles because of its hardness, strength, comparatively modest weight, and capacity for wearing smooth in use. Northwest Indians evidently recognized these attributes long ago, since they used Oregon ash for canoe paddles and digging sticks.

Naturalized Trees

The Northwest's native trees have developed into their present forms through millions of years of evolution; however their current distributions have been established only within the last 12,000 years or so, since the most recent glacial period or "ice age." Although the native trees, already described, dominate our uncultivated countryside, a few species that were introduced by man into the Northwest have escaped cultivation and become naturalized "citizens." These naturalized trees have established small, regenerating populations in the "wild," and thus might be mistaken for natives. Additionally, in the Northwest, one can find many "abandoned" trees (such as apple trees), which are not naturalized (regenerating), but may appear to be wild.

Considering the mild climate and apparently favorable growing conditions in much of the Northwest, it may seem surprising that our naturalized trees are so few and lacking in vigor. Although scores of introduced tree species thrive in cultivation, especially west of the Cascades, they are rarely able to regenerate and compete with the thriving native trees and shrubs in the surrounding forests.

One limited exception to this general rule is mazzard, the European cherry (described under "Wild Fruit Trees") that has become established in the Willamette Valley. Another is boxelder (*Acer negundo*), which is distinct in being the only maple with compound leaves (three leaflets); boxelder is native to most of the rest of the United States as well as Canada's Prairie Provinces, and it has established a few regenerating populations in various parts of the Northwest. However, our most notable naturalized trees are European mountain-ash and black locust.

The former, *Sorbus aucuparia*, is a favorite ornamental tree whose berry-like fruits are widely disseminated by birds. Thus, European mountain-ash trees occasionally grow wild, mostly near habitations, west of the Cascades.

Mountain-ashes include about 50 species of shrubs and small trees in the Northern Hemisphere. They are members of the rose family (*Rosaceae*), like most fruit trees, and are not related to the true "ashes" (*Fraxinus*). Like the ashes, they have pinnately compound leaves composed of many leaflets, but that is about the extent of the similarity; mountain-ash leaves and twigs are arranged alternately (vs. opposite in ash).

The leaves of European mountain-ash are 6 to 10 inches long and are composed of 11 to 15 sawtoothed leaflets. The number of leaflets helps distinguish this species from the two native mountain-ash shrubs (*Sorbus scopulina* and *S. sitchensis*), which have 7 to 13 leaflets. Moreover, these native shrubs are made up of several lanky stems, while European mountain-ash is distinctly tree-like with a straight trunk commonly 20 to 35 feet tall. It also has spreading boughs that support beautiful flowers or fruits much of the year.

The white mountain-ash flowers are borne in large showy flat-topped clusters. During the summer these mature into heavy, drooping masses of bright-red berry-like fruits, which are readily gobbled up by birds. Sometimes in early fall the fruits ferment and are especially sought after by flocks of waxwings, who consume too much and stagger and swoop around in a state of drunken euphoria!

Black locust (*Robinia pseudoacacia*), native to the eastern United States, has become naturalized more extensively in the Northwest than has any other tree. Its wood is very hard, tough, and decay-resistant. Because of black locust's hardiness and drought tolerance, and its value as a shade and windbreak tree as well as a source of firewood and fenceposts, it has been widely planted on farms, especially in dry country east of the Cascades. Once established, it has spread, by suckers and seed regeneration, around abandoned farmsteads and riverbanks; thus it may appear to be native.

However, there are several reasons why black locust is unlikely to be mistaken for any of our native trees. For example, it differs from all our native species in being a member of the pea

Mountain-ash in flower; black locust in flower, and seed pods

family (*Leguminosae*) and in having a legume fruit (like a pea pod) 2½ to 4 inches long. It also has distinctive compound leaves (8 to 14 inches long) made up of 11 to 21 smooth-edged leaflets. These leaves are arranged alternately on the twigs, and the base of each leaf is armed with a pair of spines ½ to 1 inch long.

Black locust can be told by its bark and its "bite." The bark is dark-colored and made up of coarse, interlacing fibrous ridges, and the "bite" has been felt by many a tree-climbing youngster who got snagged on its thorny branches.

Index